Praise For

Art of Sainthood

"Dr. Palafox is deeply aware of God and how he works in and through us. His kindness and compassion are a gift to all. Undoubtedly, his work will continue to bless others with a heightened awareness of God's pursuit of communion with his creation." —**Jonathan Hanegan**, Escuela Digital de Teología (Digital School of Theology)

"Omar Palafox masterfully bridges the divide between church and academy, providing insightful and sensitive contributions through practical theology. His work encourages meaningful dialogue that enhances both scholarly understanding and pastoral practice in the benefit of the community, fostering deeper connections between theological education and real-world ministry." —**Rev. Dr. Jessica Lugo**, Executive Director, Association for Hispanic Theological Education (AETH)

"*Art of Sainthood* invites readers to rediscover a dynamic spirituality deeply rooted in justice and social commitment. A timely book that weaves faith and action, offering a transformative framework for cultivating an authentic and engaged spiritual life." —**Harold Segura**, theologian, Baptist pastor, and Director of the Faith and Development Department of World Vision for Latin America

"In his latest book, Omar Palafox encourages readers to embrace the dynamic nature of practices and spiritual growth within our culture and experiences within the migrants' communities that can enhance our relationship with God in fullness. His approach is timely for individuals on a spiritual growth journey." —**Yenny Delgado**, Director of Publica and Convener of Women Doing Theology in Abya Yala

Art of Sainthood

Tradition and Innovation in Christian Spirituality

J. OMAR PALAFOX

ART OF SAINTHOOD
Tradition and Innovation in Christian Spirituality

ISBN 978-1-68426-024-9

Printed in the United States of America

Library of Congress Cataloging-in-Publication Data

Names: Palafox, J. Omar, author.
Title: Art of sainthood : tradition and innovation in Christian spirituality / J. Omar Palafox.
Description: Abilene, Texas : Abilene Christian University Press, [2025] | Includes bibliographical references.
Identifiers: LCCN 2025007440 (print) | LCCN 2025007441 (ebook) | ISBN 9781684260249 paperback | ISBN 9781684268580 ebook
Subjects: LCSH: Spiritual life—Christianity
Classification: LCC BV4501.3 .P337 2025 (print) | LCC BV4501.3 (ebook) | DDC 248—dc23/eng/20250715
LC record available at https://lccn.loc.gov/2025007440
LC ebook record available at https://lccn.loc.gov/2025007441

Cover design by Addie Lutzo and Molly Von Borstel, Faceout Studio
Interior text design by Scribe Inc.

For information contact:
Abilene Christian University Press
ACU Box 29138
Abilene, Texas 79699
1-877-816-4455
www.acupressbooks.com

25 26 27 28 29 30 31 / 7 6 5 4 3 2 1

To my friend Wayne Jenkins,
always a smile and J&B Coffee!
July 29, 1973–October 13, 2021
Lubbock, Texas

Contents

Part Three
Cultivating the Sacred Banquet

Boxes

Figures

Tables

Foreword

What does being a saint in the modern world mean? Is it an unattainable ideal or something ordinary people like you and me can pursue? In *Art of Sainthood*, Omar Palafox explores these questions with profound insight, weaving together his journey, cultural heritage, and deep love for Christ. From the opening chapter, you'll feel invited into a holy adventure—a journey to discover what it truly means to pursue holiness inspired by the life of Jesus.

When Omar first shared his vision for this book, I felt challenged and encouraged. This wasn't just a book I wanted to read—it was one I realized I needed for my spiritual journey.

Through themes like Majesty, Piety, Solitude, and Rectitude, Omar invites readers to cultivate Christlike character while pursuing justice-oriented living. Drawing on his experiences as a missionary and professor, he introduces readers to the treasures of Latin American spirituality. Figures like de las Casas, Romero, and Gutiérrez come alive alongside transformative concepts like *abuelita* theology, liberation theology, and *misión integral.*

What I love about Omar's writing is his ability to blend theology with poetry and history with personal experience. His words don't just inform—they inspire. Reading this book feels like sitting across from a trusted mentor who speaks with conviction and compassion.

Omar's bicultural perspective, shaped by his roots in Latin America and the United States, enriches this book remarkably. He bridges the wisdom of Latin American spirituality—grounded in communal, justice-oriented faith—with the Western emphasis on personal growth and theological precision. This well-rounded perspective makes the book a gift to readers of all backgrounds, demonstrating how diverse expressions of faith can deepen and challenge one another.

His reflections on justice are central, rooted in Scripture and lived experience. With a storyteller's voice, Omar draws on personal and cultural narratives, weaving in poetic insights that bring his teachings to life.

Omar's deep connection to his roots and commitment to speaking into today's world testify to his authenticity. He and his family live out *mi casa es tu casa*, offering hospitality, fostering a sense of belonging, and creating joyful spaces. Rooted in his Mexican heritage, this way of life reflects a Kingdom-shaped perspective that joyfully welcomes others and celebrates life in the community.

One of the most moving aspects of this book is its reminder that sainthood is cultivated in everyday people's small, faithful acts. When Omar highlights the quiet prayers of a grandmother and the sacrificial love of a mother, he reminds us that sainthood isn't reserved for the extraordinary but lived out in the ordinary moments of grace, humility, and loving resilience. This is what shapes the heart of this book: the profound truth that sainthood is within reach for all who pursue a life marked by love and justice in everyday life.

As Dallas Willard states, "The true saint burns grace like a 747 jet burns fuel on takeoff," highlighting how deeply dependent a Christlike life is on God's abundant grace.[1] Similarly, Thomas Merton emphasizes that sainthood involves simply becoming the person God created us to be: "For me to be a saint means to be myself."[2] Léon Bloy poignantly captures the urgency of this calling: "The only real sadness, the only real failure, the only great tragedy in life, is not to become a saint."[3]

Omar's credentials are as impressive as his character. Recently honored as Professor of the Year at Abilene Christian University, his excellence as a teacher and scholar is widely recognized. Yet beyond academia, his faith and influence stretch across continents, leaving a lasting impact wherever he goes. What sets Omar apart is how he lives what he teaches. His life is a relentless embodiment of the grace, justice, and love he calls others to pursue.

In a world too often marked by division, injustice, and spiritual restlessness, this book offers a timely reminder that holiness is not just a personal pursuit; it is a call to make a difference in the world. Omar connects timeless biblical truths with today's pressing issues—such as poverty, migration, and systemic inequality—offering a path forward rooted in reflection and action. Omar has a remarkable gift for listening deeply to the voices of the marginalized, amplifying their stories with dignity and power, and weaving them into the fabric of God's redemptive narrative. Through his work of listening, he shows how the wisdom of the overlooked can transform how we understand faith, community, and justice.

Omar and I have been amigos for thirty years, and throughout our journey together, I've been deeply inspired by his unwavering gaze fixed on Jesus. His greatest desire is to know Christ, love Him fully, and reflect His presence in every aspect of life.

As you read *Art of Sainthood*, you may be inspired to walk the path of everyday sainthood—not in isolation but in community. May you be nourished by God's sustaining grace.

May you pursue justice with courage and neighborly love.

This is more than just a book to read—it is an invitation to embody God's vision for the world by following Jesus's example.

¡Buen provecho!

James Henderson
Cofounder and codirector of *Ashrei*:
Centro de Formación Espiritual
Ciudad de México

Acknowledgments

Creating this book was anything but a solo effort—it was an actual group project built on years of spiritual growth, encouragement, and collaboration. This work results from countless hours spent researching, discussing, and writing, and I am incredibly grateful to everyone who contributed to its creation.

First and foremost, I am thankful for my family, who were my foundation through it all. Their belief in me and endless patience kept me going. To my spouse, Tana, thank you for understanding my late nights and long hours spent thinking and writing. You brought laughter and perspective when things got complicated. To my kids, Xitlali and Gonzalo, thank you for filling my days with joy and curiosity. *Y mi hermana querida, Barbara, gracias.*

I thank my editor, Jason Fikes, who initially believed in this project. His keen insights, thoughtful suggestions, and talent for refining my ideas made this book unique. I am also grateful to Mary V. McCracken, a spiritual mentor and friend who helped me see beauty in vulnerability and growth. My friend James Henderson deserves a big thank-you too. He has added depth and warmth to our shared spiritual pilgrimage, creating a wonderful atmosphere of support and friendship for our families.

My most profound appreciation goes to Dr. Urban T. Holmes, who sparked my love for this work and helped shape my thinking. His influence has been a guiding light in creating this book. I am also thankful to my colleagues and friends who provided valuable feedback and insights that enriched this work. Special thanks to Nora Kviatkovski, a dear friend who has walked with me through the highs and lows of this spiritual pilgrimage.

I would also like to thank my colleagues at Abilene Christian University for their support and the many authors, scholars, and researchers whose work has been the foundation of my research. Without their dedication, this book would not be what it is today.

Finally, thank you to all the readers who helped me with this work. I hope it brings you as much joy and inspiration as I found while writing it. Any imperfections are mine, but the true essence of this book is thanks to everyone mentioned here and so many others who have enriched my life in countless ways.

Introduction

Creating a Robust Spiritual Diet

God is not a hypothesis derived from logical assumptions, but an immediate insight, self-evident as light. He is not something to be sought in the darkness with the light of reason. He is light.

—Abraham and Susannah Heschel

Sainthood should not be a remote designation applicable only to exceptional Christians. It should be an accessible, dynamic spiritual trajectory open to all. Personal spiritual growth and communal transformation are possible only if we reimagine the foundations of holiness.

Samin Nosrat, the celebrated chef and author, revolutionized cooking for at-home chefs with her simple, intuitive framework of salt, fat, acid, and heat. She revealed to millions how they could become more competent in the kitchen and understand how recipes combine these essential aspects to create depth and proportion. For Nosrat, culinary success hinges on the interplay between these pillars.[1] Four building blocks sustain the Christian life: **Majesty**, which honors God's authority; **Piety**, which practices daily devotion and service; **Solitude**, which enhances reflective clarity; and **Rectitude**, which embodies just relationships. The interplay of **MPSR** constantly balances and reshapes the saint's spirituality to cultivate an intentional, transformative faith.

Our familiarity and comprehensive engagement with these four revolutionary theological ideas can lead to the art of sainthood. Whether you are just beginning your spiritual pilgrimage or are a seasoned practitioner, I invite you to reassess your spiritual diet and discover how to create a more robust, nourishing, and fulfilling spiritual life together.

Like any culinary artist skillfully blending diverse ingredients, spiritual growth requires the interplay of tradition, creativity, discipline, and communal wisdom and yields the resilient, transformative nourishment that comes from cultivating a relationship with God. Integrating spiritual formation with social praxis highlights how theological foundations are not merely abstract concepts but vital guides for addressing the church's social responsibility and individual well-being. These principles call for practical application within contemporary society, urging believers to connect spiritual growth with active social engagement. This interconnected approach aligns with the broader goals of movements in Latine theology despite the historical suspicion these perspectives have faced.

Engaging with other disciplines, like philosophy, has long been a part of theological discourse, and modern theologians engage with contemporary intellectual currents. This adaptability supports the embrace of Latine theology as a response to the pressing questions posed: *How can the church align itself with history and address the needs of the people?* This question extends beyond church authorities, inviting all saints to actively participate in addressing social responsibility and personal spiritual formation.

Prominent evangelical figures like Pedro Arana, Samuel Escobar, and René Padilla—alongside Gustavo Gutiérrez, Jon Sobrino, and Ignacio Ellacuría from the Catholic tradition—pioneered practical theology in Latin America, forming the theological underpinnings that integrate spiritual formation with social praxis.[2] They followed a tradition of engagement inspired by figures such as Ignacio de Loyola, Juan de la Cruz, Teresa of Ávila, and Bartolomé de las Casas, whose works, while sometimes censored, laid the groundwork for a spiritually vibrant and socially engaged theology.

Escobar and Padilla, for example, framed their Christological reflection around the concepts of incarnation, cross, and resurrection, urging believers to imitate Jesus in his earthly mission. This theological frame parallels the foundations of spiritual formation, which require believers to probe history, challenge obstacles, and engage with the lived realities of people in communities facing oppression—in Latin America and globally. Ellacuría, Gutiérrez, and others elaborated with Marxism and social sciences on what is referred to as liberation theology.

Box I.1 The Core Ingredients of a Christian Life

Saints throughout history have refined their souls by communing with God. As we nourish our spirits, like chefs cooking, we build on essential elements that interplay with our link with God and guide us toward our spiritual purpose.

- **Majesty (M)** acknowledges God's sacred authority over daily actions. This foundational element calls us to honor God's sovereignty, infusing our lives with purpose and humility. Like salt in a dish, **Majesty** enhances the flavor of every other spiritual practice, bringing depth and structure. Without it, our spiritual life would lack direction and grounding.
- **Piety (P)** embodies the role of the priest as we intervene in the lives of others. It connects us to God through daily devotion, prayer, and compassionate service. **Piety** is like the fat in a recipe—it enriches and sustains our faith, adding warmth and fullness to our spiritual life. Without it, our faith would feel dry and lifeless, but with it, our hearts become generous and open to God's presence.
- **Solitude (S)** mirrors the wisdom of the mystic. It provides space for reflection, cutting through the distractions of daily life to reveal spiritual clarity. Like acid in a meal, **Solitude** sharpens our focus, helping us see our lives and God's work with fresh eyes. Our spiritual vision may become dull without it, but with it we gain profound insight and inner peace.
- **Rectitude (R)** reflects the strength of the warrior. It promotes ethical living rooted in just relationships and discipline. **Rectitude** is like heat in cooking—without it, the other ingredients would not hold. True righteousness involves practical actions that support fairness and justice in our interactions with others.

The amalgamation of spirituality and resistance is also vividly expressed in the cultural works of Latin American theologians and artists. The *misa campesina* (peasants' mass) in Nicaragua and the *misa criolla* (creole mass) in Argentina stand as artistic and spiritual responses to oppression, much like the revolutionary expressions of music, poetry, and murals found in the works of Mercedes Sosa, Ernesto Cardenal, Facundo Cabral, Violeta Parra, and others.[3] These cultural forms serve as acts of defiance against oppressive systems, embodying the theological principles of spiritual formation.

Box I.2 Music as Resistance

Composed in the 1960s by Ariel Ramírez, **misa criolla** fuses Catholic liturgy with Andean folk music, using Indigenous instruments and rhythms. It is a celebrated expression of spiritual and cultural hybridity in Latin America.

Composed in the 1970s by Carlos Mejía Godoy, **misa campesina** blends Catholic liturgy with Nicaraguan peasant struggles, folk music, and political themes from the Sandinista Revolution. It reflects the deep bond between faith and social justice in marginalized Latin American communities.

The 1965 Delano Grape Strike, led by César Chávez and Dolores Huerta, began as a labor strike by the Agricultural Workers Organizing Committee and was later joined by the United Farm Workers. Predominantly involving Mexican and Filipino farmworkers, it demanded better wages and working conditions. A pivotal moment in the US farmworkers' rights movement, it exemplified the intersection of labor rights, social justice, and nonviolent activism. The struggle for justice was about workers' rights and the sacredness of Creation. I have learned that true spirituality is a woven thread—where personal devotion and collective justice are bound together, strengthening the other in lived action.

I have chosen to refer to this heritage as Latine theology, which emerged from a liminal space shaped by the interplay of colonial and colonized elements. It exists in a dynamic process of negotiation and synthesis. Rooted in Indigenous, African, and European influences, Latine theology resists binary categorizations. It reciprocally engages in global theological discourse, drawing from and enriching it with unique contributions from its hybrid identity. The concept of the "Brown Church," as articulated by Robert Chao Romero, highlights the distinctive voice of Latine communities in confronting colonial legacies and advocating for justice and liberation for over five hundred years.[4] Historians like Juan Miguel Zunzunegui who are reexamining the narrative of the Spanish *Conquista* are reshaping how this history is taught, challenging long-standing Eurocentric perspectives.[5] This ongoing historical reflection exemplifies how theological principles, especially within the liminality of the Latine tradition, must continually evolve to engage with the complexities of history, ensuring they remain relevant, transformative, and rooted in justice.

The Brown Church offers a critical framework for addressing social and historical injustices, demonstrating that theology is not static but must respond to marginalized communities' lived experiences and historical realities.

Applying theology means confronting hard questions, engaging history, and embodying Christ's call to renewal. Latine theology offers a rich foundation for personal growth, communal empowerment, resisting oppression, and seeking justice. As Carmen Nanko-Fernández explores in *Theologizing en Espanglish*, US Latine theological reflections emerge from the lived realities of marginalized communities, embracing a contextual, communal, and practical approach that challenges dominant ecclesial and social norms.[6] These traditions invite us to a spirituality of action—a faith that stews in lived experience and moves toward liberation and restoration, just as Christ did.

Criticism of Rolheiser's Four Pillars

Ronald Rolheiser's four pillars of spirituality have faced criticism from various groups. Traditionalists argue that his views on sexuality, influenced by Freudian elements, may diverge from orthodox Catholic teachings, while some academics suggest his approach challenges established doctrine and lacks spiritual depth. These critiques reflect differing theological and ideological perspectives. My exploration of essential elements of the Christian faith builds on such ongoing discussions. In the *Holy Longing*, Rolheiser identifies four foundational pillars of a healthy Christian spiritual life: prayer and private morality, social justice, mellowness of heart, and community involvement.[7] These pillars form a solid foundation for spiritual, moral, social, and communal life, aiding believers in balancing personal devotion with societal engagement. However, it is essential to note that this valuable framework (and others like Foster's Six Streams)[8] has been critiqued for not fully addressing the sociopolitical and cultural contexts experienced by marginalized communities, thereby highlighting the need for a more comprehensive approach.

While Rolheiser's framework balances personal transformation and community involvement, it often falls short in addressing the sociopolitical dimensions that Latine theologies emphasize. In Rolheiser's reality, it may have worked, but for me, it does not. These movements call for an individual and communal spirituality integrating righteous anger, contextual engagement, and prophetic resistance to systemic injustice.

Through the lens of Latine theology, Carmen Nanko-Fernández writes that a more robust spirituality emerges for everybody who directly engages with contextual theology and stresses the importance of *convivencia*—cohabitation and shared living—which promotes a theology embedded in community life.[9] Liberation theology, expressed by theologians like Gutiérrez (and others) and Padilla,[10] emphasizes that genuine Christian spirituality must be grounded in solidarity and conscientization with people facing oppression and the gospel. Gutiérrez's concept of the "preferential option for the poor" insists that Christian spirituality is not simply a moral position but a call to direct action for systemic change.[11] This call to action should make us all feel the urgency for change. Leonardo Boff expands this vision by including ecological concerns, arguing that the liberation of those lacking is interconnected with the liberation of the earth; Pablo Richard and Enrique Dussel echo this sentiment.[12] We can see these critiques point out that Rolheiser's spirituality, while valuable, remains too general and detached from the concrete struggles of reality lived in specific communities. For liberation theology, spirituality must be intrinsically political and embodied in communal resistance, as highlighted by theologians like José Miguez Bonino, who emphasizes the importance of communitarian spiritual expressions such as rituals, art, and music.[13]

Additionally, Elsa Támez and Ivone Gebara emphasize that justice requires not just personal moral responses but collective action aimed at dismantling patriarchal, racialized, and capitalist systems of inequality.[14] These theologians emphasize that the gospel calls for individual and social transformation, addressing people's spiritual and material needs. *Misión integral* also critiques Rolheiser's focus on private morality and prayer, advocating for a spirituality that directly engages with ingrained injustices like poverty and inequality by insisting that personal holiness must be lived out in the public sphere, challenging unjust social, political, and economic structures. While Rolheiser's framework seeks inner peace, *misión integral* argues that righteous anger against injustice can be essential for spiritual growth.

Latine theologies, including Pentecostalism, stress the need for contextual theology, where spirituality responds to the social and economic realities in which people live. Rolheiser's framework, while offering a balanced road map for living out faith, does not fully address the need for contextual engagement with historical and cultural struggles. Liberation theology emphasizes that

Box I.3 The Micah Declaration and *Misión Integral*

Adopted in 2001 by the Micah network, this declaration affirms that the Christian mission integrates gospel proclamation and social action, emphasizing justice for the poor and oppressed as essential to faith. This perspective insists that gospel proclamation inherently carries social implications, while social action testifies to Christ's transformative grace, rejecting any divide between spiritual and material needs.

Misión integral, "the proclamation and demonstration of the gospel," affirms the church's role in pursuing Christ's peace and justice, particularly for the poor and oppressed.

Colombian historian Salinas traces the roots of *misión integral* to Latin American theologians Padilla and Escobar. See Salinas, *Latin American Evangelical Theology in the 1970s: The Golden Decade* (Langham Monographs, 2009); and Sharon E. Heaney, *Contextual Theology for Latin America: Liberation Themes in Evangelical Perspective* (Wipf & Stock, 2008).

the lived experiences of individuals from marginalized backgrounds should shape spirituality. At the same time, *misión integral* advocates for a holistic mission that integrates evangelism with relational justice, calling believers to ground their spirituality in practical actions that support fair treatment, uplift communities, and challenge unjust structures.

Orlando E. Costas, another key figure in *misión integral*, argues that evangelism must be contextual and speak to individual and communal needs.[15] Costas's critique of a universalized spirituality aligns with liberation theology's commitment to grounding the Christian mission in the struggles of people facing oppression in their communities. Both perspectives emphasize the need for a contextualized faith that responds to the specific realities of marginalized groups rather than a one-size-fits-all approach, affirming the church's role in advocating for justice and liberation. In contrast, Rolheiser's framework does not sufficiently engage with how ingrained injustices shape spiritual routines and communal life.

Rolheiser's emphasis on "mellowness of heart" focuses on inner peace and compassion for personal spiritual growth. However, theologians of the liberation theology tradition like Ellacuría, Juan Luis Segundo, and Jon Sobrino assert that spirituality must include righteous anger and prophetic resistance to oppression.[16] Marcella Althaus-Reid adds that emotional tranquility may not always be the proper response for marginalized communities.[17] Latine theology argues that personal morality and spirituality must lead to active engagement with social transformation, sometimes necessitating righteous anger and resistance to systemic injustice.

Viewed through the lenses of these Latine concepts, Rolheiser's four pillars provide a good starting point, but they must be strengthened with a more profound commitment to systemic justice, communal resistance, and societal transformation. These theological traditions argue that authentic Christian spirituality must not only nurture personal holiness but also empower individuals and communities to participate in the holistic mission of the gospel, advancing both personal and social transformation according to reality.

Mestizo Pilgrimage

I identify as a bridge between cultures—a Mexican born in Guadalajara and now part of the Hispanic diaspora in the United States—embracing the richness of a hybrid identity (or mestizo) that combines deep-rooted traditions with a dynamic, cross-cultural perspective. Rooted in my Mexican heritage and shaped by the hyphenated life of a Hispanic in the United States, this exploration reflects my blend of identities and missionary experiences. Racial terms are imperfect—Hispanic is broad, and mestizo/a reflects mixed ancestry—so I use Latine for inclusivity and cultural diversity, recognizing how diverse traditions shape Latine theology.

After conducting a DNA test to explore my heritage, I discovered that I am 42 percent Spaniard and 38 percent Mexican Indigenous, with the remaining percentage a blend of other ancestries. This revelation was a surprise and a profound moment of self-discovery, highlighting the uniquely hyphenated nature of my identity as both Spaniard and Indigenous—a unique fusion that shapes my personal and cultural perspective.

Therefore, I approach sainthood through a lens of cultural hybridity, merging diverse artistic elements, traditions, and principles into a uniquely transformative whole. Embracing this rich spiritual heritage affirms that spiritual wholeness is a dynamic, accessible pilgrimage that transcends geographic

Table I.1 Comparative Analysis of Christian Spirituality

Dimensions	Rolheiser's Four Pillars	Liberation Theology	*Misión Integral*
Personal Spirituality vs. Communal Praxis	Focuses on personal spirituality, with some emphasis on community involvement but less on systemic change. Spirituality is often about personal transformation and balance.	Focuses on communal spirituality rooted in solidarity with the poor and people facing oppression, with an emphasis on communal resistance as key to spiritual life.	Emphasizes the integration of personal spirituality and social justice, advocating for both individual transformation and communal engagement in addressing systemic injustice.
Holistic Spirituality vs. Righteous Anger	Emphasizes mellowness of heart and balance, focusing on inner peace and integration rather than righteous anger as a spiritual response to injustice.	Stresses the necessity of righteous anger in the face of systemic injustice, viewing it as a vital spiritual response rather than focusing solely on inner peace.	Recognizes that righteous anger can be a necessary spiritual response to systemic injustice, focusing on both spiritual and social transformation.
Engaging with Historical and Cultural Context	Engages with modern human experiences and longings but offers a generalized approach to spirituality without focusing on historical or cultural oppression.	Deeply contextual, focusing on historical and cultural realities of marginalized communities, particularly in relation to oppression and poverty.	Focuses on contextual mission, urging the church to engage with the specific social, political, and economic challenges of each community.
Spirituality as Prophetic Resistance	Focuses more on personal morality and compassion, with less emphasis on direct resistance to oppression or systemic injustice.	Emphasizes spirituality as a form of prophetic resistance against systems of injustice, with a strong focus on liberation and social transformation.	Sees spirituality as prophetic and mission oriented, emphasizing the need for active engagement in challenging and transforming unjust systems.

Box I.4 Key Terms in Latine Communities

Latino/Latina refers to people of Latin American descent, while **Latinx/Latine** are gender-neutral alternatives.

Chicano/Chicana denotes Mexican Americans, often with political ties, and **Tejano/Tejana** specifies those in Texas.

Pocho/Pocha can imply disconnection from Mexican roots.

Hispanic covers Spanish-speaking peoples, while **mestizo/mestiza** refers to mixed European and Indigenous heritage.

Afro-Latino/Afro-Latina highlights African ancestry. These terms reflect the diversity within Latine identities.

and cultural boundaries, inviting all into communion with God and a commitment to transformative societal change.

In a world marked by fragmentation and a deep search for meaning, this work provides a cohesive framework that integrates ancient wisdom with fresh perspectives—particularly relevant for multicultural and interfaith communities. Rooting spirituality in cultural hybridity and honoring core principles, it confronts the realities of injustice, isolation, and spiritual malnourishment, echoing Elizabeth Conde-Frazier's vision of spirituality as a response to and relationship with God, revealed in Scripture and embodied in Jesus Christ.[18] Just as our bodies crave nourishment, our souls require a richer "diet" for proper sustenance—one shaped by patient mastery of foundational practices and enriched by a Mexican and Latine heritage that informs theological reflection and action.

Every foundation cultivates our bond with the Creator. This pilgrimage emphasizes the path itself, not just the destination. Seeking these four fundamental elements of spirituality provides a strong rule of life for spiritual fulfillment, enabling individuals to become Spirit-led, creative, and effective faith practitioners. John Donne's insight that "no man is an island" and Thomas Merton's reflections on interconnectedness reveal a profound truth about the nature of spirituality: It cannot exist only in isolation.[19] Donne's words in *For Whom the Bell Tolls* remind us that everyone's life is tied to the greater whole, echoing Merton's belief in our shared responsibility for one another.[20] The preferential option for the poor—a foundational principle of Latine theology—can serve as a guiding lens for nurturing a holistic and personalized spiritual life. This perspective facilitates a more resonant communion with God while inspiring meaningful societal transformation. Recognizing that personal faith and communal well-being are intricately intertwined, we embark on spiritual pilgrimages that unfold individually and collectively.

Box I.5 More Key Terms

The term **saint** broadly refers to those considered holy or virtuous across religious traditions. In **Catholicism**, saints are canonized and believed to be in heaven, while in **many Protestant traditions**, the term applies to all believers. This book uses an inclusive, nondenominational approach to refer to individuals recognized for holiness or virtue.

The Second Vatican Council (1962–65) laid the foundation for **liberation theology** by emphasizing the church's responsibility to social justice and the poor. Documents like *Gaudium et spes* and *Lumen gentium* underscored the church's mission to defend human dignity and the universal call to holiness, affirming that all believers are called to be saints through daily engagement with the world. These teachings influenced theologians such as **Gutiérrez**, who reframed theology through the lens of social and economic justice; **Boff**, who critiqued oppressive political systems; **Sobrino**, who saw the suffering Christ as a model for solidarity with the marginalized; **Segundo**, who emphasized theology from the perspective of the oppressed; and **Romero**, who denounced the violent repression of the poor in El Salvador. Rooted in Vatican II, their work reinforced the inseparability of faith and justice.

Christian Rule of Life is a structured spiritual practice that enhances growth and faithful living. Rooted in Scripture and tradition, it includes prayer, worship, study, and service. Examples include the Rule of St. Benedict and modern adaptations.

Preferential option for the poor is a core principle of **liberation theology**; it emphasizes God's special concern for the marginalized and the call to prioritize their needs. Theologians like **Gutiérrez** stress that faith must be lived out in solidarity with the poor, addressing systemic injustice and working toward liberation.

Grounded in wisdom, we blend time-honored traditions with innovative spiritual practices to create a spirituality that actively addresses pressing societal challenges, such as justice and liberation. This approach underscores the profound interdependence of faith, wisdom, and transformative action, since it is not a set way of seeing the other or God. From this perspective, Bonino's theology powerfully writes about the idea that personal faith and communal flourishing are intertwined.[21] Faith interspersed into daily life transforms the soul and society, revealing that personal devotion ignites communal renewal.[22] In the following chapters, we will explore these elements in greater depth through the lives and expressions of saints.

Spiritual Growth as a Creative Cultural Process

Latin America and the Caribbean, currently home to 662 million people (representing 8.2 percent of the global population), are projected to reach 752 million by 2056, while the Hispanic/Latine population in the United States exceeds 63.6 million.[23] These figures highlight the urgent need to understand Latine spirituality through formal doctrine and lived faith, communal bonds, and the fusion of Indigenous, Catholic, and evangelical practices.[24] I have found that spirituality flourishes when tradition meets innovation and is shaped by community and culture. As Héctor Varela-Rios suggests, human existence is an act of *sancochar*, a dynamic stew where tradition and new expressions mingle, forging an ever-evolving faith enriched by heritage and personal engagement.[25] Like *sancochar*, my spiritual growth continually blends, contests, and transforms through diverse cultural influences. Much like a chef blending time-honored recipes with new flavors, believers fine-tune their spiritual "diets," discovering depth through patient discernment and reverence. Spirituality, like *sancochar*, is not static—it requires mixing, wrestling, and transformation.

In this evolving landscape, **Majesty** grounds believers in God's authority, **Piety** enriches faith through devotion and service, **Solitude** sharpens reflective clarity, and **Rectitude** sustains just relationships—an interplay reminiscent of Latin America's cultural hybridity. Liberation theology, born in these hybrid spaces, reframes sanctity as communal solidarity with the marginalized and invites contemplation and action. Resilience and adaptability, woven through Latin American history, mirror how spirituality is passed down, each generation refining it with fresh insights.

Spiritual practices remain vital as regional cuisines merge Spanish, African, and Indigenous influences. They incorporate new ideas while honoring core traditions. Culinary metaphors illustrate how shared meals nurture communal identity, and spiritual practices similarly cultivate our bond with God and one another. Ondina and Justo González show how Latin American churches integrate inherited customs with innovative expressions.[26] In cuisine and faith, this ongoing process ensures a dynamic, purposeful, and transformative pilgrimage rooted in the essential "ingredients" of Christian life.

My Story: A Blend of Tradition and Innovation

My Catholic education, shaped by structured rituals and sacred traditions, laid the foundation for my spiritual formation and intellectual growth. Regular attendance at Mass, daily prayer, and a rich liturgical life instilled in me a profound reverence for the sacred. Over time, I witnessed how Pope Paul VI's *Evangelii nuntiandi* underscores the gospel's universal scope while championing its dynamic engagement with diverse cultures, reminding us that no single culture can exhaust the fullness of the Good News.[27] As the gospel encounters different contexts, fresh insights emerge, much like the interplay between the solemnity of Catholic Mass, the impassioned worship of Pentecostalism, and the scriptural devotion of the Churches of Christ.

As a mestizo missionary, I have come to view spirituality—like culinary traditions—as contextual and ever-evolving. Drawing on *mestizaje*, a concept explored by Latino theologians such as Virgilio Elizondo, I see cultural and spiritual hybridity as a source of depth and vitality.[28] Likewise, as Óscar Garcia-Johnson highlights, embracing a richly "mestizo" spirituality sustains a deeply contextual, relational understanding of the gospel.[29] Navigating multiple identities allows faith, justice, and liberation to intersect naturally, reflecting how spirituality expands through diverse influences and expressions. Additionally, Saint Augustine's *City of God* (*De Civitate Dei*), which probes the boundary between the sacred and secular, has guided my understanding of hybrid identities and cultures.[30]

In pursuing this evolving spirituality, I have discovered how **Majesty** (honoring God's sovereign presence), **Piety** (cultivating humble devotion), **Solitude** (creating space for introspection and renewal), and **Rectitude** (living with integrity and moral courage) offer a solid framework that unites structure with openness. I have learned that sainthood blooms in the daily rhythms of life, where tradition, culture, and faith intertwine. As I grow in compassion and service, these roots shape my pilgrimage and our shared mission.

Our Look Ahead

This work presents the pilgrimage toward sainthood as dynamic and adaptable. Drawing on St. Teresa of Ávila's reforms, which emphasized spiritual flexibility, I propose that adaptability cultivates rather than diminishes our bond with God. Grounded in theological wisdom yet open to new experiences, this "new diet" provides a practical framework for discerning God's call while honoring sacred tradition.

The opening chapters introduce four theological foundations, highlighting their historical and cultural significance, particularly within Latine spirituality. Chapter Four addresses **Majesty** through Teresa of Ávila, whose profound spiritual experiences and reforms underscore how recognizing God's sovereign authority upholds personal and communal transformation. Her example in Spain demonstrates that acknowledging sacred authority equips believers to lead with conviction and purpose, prompting reflection on how God's **Majesty** can shape our lives.

Chapter Five turns to **Piety**, exemplified by Bartolomé de las Casas. His humble life of service illustrates how daily devotion nurtures spiritual growth, primarily through advocacy for those facing oppression in Latin America. By integrating service into their spiritual practice, believers strengthen their relationship with God and others, advancing devotion and justice. Chapter Six explores **Solitude**, as seen in Juan de la Cruz. His introspective spirituality reveals that **Solitude** is not isolation but a path to renewal and clarity, inviting readers to consider how intentional stillness supports deeper self-awareness and a more profound tie to the transcendent—an approach deeply resonant with Latine traditions that weave introspection into daily devotion. Chapter Seven examines **Rectitude**, focusing on Ignacio de Loyola, whose disciplined lifestyle and Jesuit foundations model steadfast integrity and relational justice. His leadership amid adversity mirrors the Latine community's persistent pursuit of justice, urging readers to uphold moral courage and ethical relationships in tangible, practical ways.

This book also features *cuentos*—narratives akin to parables—that convey practical wisdom enriched by cultural heritage (magical realism). They illuminate the interplay between intellect, emotion, and celestial revelation, challenging readers to adapt and refine their spiritual commitments, much like adjusting the ingredients of a well-crafted diet. Interplaying together four core virtues—**Majesty**, **Piety**, **Solitude**, and **Rectitude**—these pages outline a road map for accessible sainthood. Far from an unreachable ideal, sainthood emerges here as an ongoing pilgrimage that aligns us with God's mission of justice and transformation, empowering us to be agents of liberation and spiritual flourishing within our communities.

Part One

Nourishing the Soul through a Spiritual Diet

Through his honor and glory he has given us his precious and wonderful promises, that you may share the divine nature and escape from the world's immorality that sinful craving produces.

—Apostle Peter (2 Pet. 1:4 CEB)

Chapter One

How a Robust Spiritual Diet Can Feed the Soul

Modern man listens more willingly to witnesses than to teachers, and if he does listen to teachers, it is because they are witnesses.

—Pope Paul VI

In 1949, in the mountainous region of Zacatecas, Mexico, a young woman faced a profound ordeal. Laboring alone, she delivered a stillborn baby. Desperate and without support, she turned to her faith, covering the lifeless infant in honey and fervently praying to the Virgin of Guadalupe. Against all odds, her prayers were answered as the baby began to cry. In gratitude, she named him Guadalupe after the Virgin, who had intervened in her darkest hour. Known to the community as Lupe (my father), his life as a church planter and disciple-maker in the churches of Christ became a testament to the transformative power of faith and grace.

In the story of Guadalupe, I have learned a lesson for all faith communities: Christ's message takes root in culture, testimony transforms lives, and inclusive ministry flourishes when faith speaks in the people's language. The story illustrates the principle of incarnational and contextualized faith, demonstrating how Christ's message becomes transformative when rooted in cultural identity, lived testimony, and inclusive ministry.

Lupe's narrative reveals that God is present in extraordinary miracles and everyday moments of life. His birth, an otherwise ordinary event, became a profound supernatural encounter. Lupe's life exemplifies how the sacred can transform the mundane (*lo cotidiano*), turning even the most painful experiences into moments of grace.[1] His story embodies Pope Paul VI's words:

"Modern man listens more willingly to witnesses than to teachers, and if he does listen to teachers, it is because they are witnesses."[2] Lupe's humble acts of kindness and unwavering devotion bore witness to the real impact of faith—his life itself was a sermon.[3]

The Virgin of Guadalupe holds deep cultural and theological significance. Elizondo highlights her role in shaping a new mestizo identity,[4] while Roberto Goizueta emphasizes her call to an embodied faith of accompaniment.[5] Jeanette Rodríguez underscores her power as a source of resilience and justice.[6] For Lupe's mother, Guadalupe was not just a religious figure but a symbol of hope in hardship, revealing God's presence in the ordinary. Inspired by this faith, Lupe dedicated his life to church planting, embodying humility, compassion, and service—the heart of spiritual fulfillment.

This chapter explores how consistent, thoughtful spiritual practices encourage transformative growth, nourishing the individual soul and the broader community. The Virgin's role in Lupe's story reflects the spiritual sustenance available through tradition, reminding us that faith, much like food, nourishes both body and soul. Lupe's life exemplifies how the critical elements of a spiritual diet—faith, service, and devotion—bolster resilience and cultivate one's tie with God, rendering the everyday sacred.

A robust spiritual life flourishes by integrating diverse traditions and rituals, enriching the soul, and developing holistic growth. Lupe's story demonstrates that sainthood is not reserved for those performing extraordinary miracles but is accessible to all who live with intention, faith, and service. We cultivate resilience and adaptability in our spiritual lives by integrating spiritual applications from different cultures. Christianity, shaped by culture, finds its expression in the rich interplay of traditions across the globe. This dynamic blending nourishes the soul, allowing us to grow spiritually while honoring cultural diversity.

The Central Question

The tension between critiques of Latine theology and spirituality—particularly in the context of oppression, exploitation, and the preferential option for the poor—reveals a profound theological conflict. At the heart of this tension lies the challenge of integrating traditional spiritual insights with the lived realities of systemic injustice. Liberation theology emphasizes Jesus's incarnation among individuals from marginalized backgrounds, portraying him as a companion in suffering. This resonates closely with those facing oppression in Latin America during the mid-twentieth century.

To better understand the dynamic interplay of Latine theology and spirituality within the **MPSR** framework, examining two contrasting figures, Horacio Bojorge and Rutilio Grande, is insightful. Bojorge is a contemporary Jesuit theologian from Uruguay known for emphasizing traditional Catholic teachings, prayerful spirituality, and strict adherence to orthodox doctrine. He is particularly critical of liberation theology, believing it risks losing sight of deeper spiritual traditions by focusing too much on earthly struggles.[7] He has argued that authentic spiritual growth must prioritize reverence for God's divine majesty and engage in reflective prayer rather than be overly involved in temporary political issues.

On the other hand, Grande (1928–77), a Jesuit priest from El Salvador, exemplified integrating another type of spirituality with active social justice efforts. Grande lived among and served rural poor communities, focusing on social justice and advocating for the rights and dignity of marginalized groups.[8] His faith was personal and reflective and actively shaped his commitment to confronting injustice and oppression. Grande exemplified **Rectitude** by courageously speaking out against injustice, even at the risk of his life—he was assassinated because of his work. His life demonstrates that spirituality involves inner contemplation and outward social transformation, a fundamental principle in liberation theology.

These two figures highlight a key tension within Latine theology and spirituality. Bojorge urges caution, emphasizing preserving spiritual depth and doctrinal fidelity. Grande, meanwhile, shows that spirituality and social activism can and should coexist, demonstrating that faith becomes most meaningful when it actively seeks justice and transformation in the world. Both perspectives significantly shape the ongoing dialogue and development of Latine theological thought. The **MPSR** framework effectively addresses this tension by uniting traditional spiritual practices with the reality of systemic injustice, guiding believers toward a balanced, contemplative, and socially transformative faith.

The Galilean Journey

The concept of a Galilean journey is a compelling metaphor for cultivating a robust spiritual diet, emphasizing that genuine spiritual nourishment often emerges from the margins, where diverse cultures intersect. Like Jesus's time through Galilee, as articulated by Elizondo, contemporary Christianity draws strength from encounters at the peripheries.[9] Galilee, shaped by a confluence of Jewish, Gentile, and Roman influences, demonstrates how cultural hybridity can enrich spiritual life. This concept invites us to blend ancient wisdom with modern experiences, creating a multifaceted approach to spiritual nourishment that mirrors Jesus's path through Galilee—one that embraces tradition while being transformed by God's grace.

Elizondo's portrayal of Jesus as the "marginal Jew" highlights the importance of embracing diversity in spiritual practices. As Galilee was a space where different cultures met to create something new, our spiritual lives should also draw from diverse traditions to enrich the soul. This inclusivity reflects Jesus's ministry, urging us to grow spiritually in diverse perspectives—whether through contemplative prayer, Indigenous wisdom, or acts of service.[10] We often encounter the heavenly profoundly and unexpectedly by embracing these marginal spaces.

Ellacuría's emphasis on praxis aligns with Jesus's ministry in Galilee, which unfolded on the fringes of society.[11] Ellacuría suggests that significant spiritual insights often arise from marginalized communities. He posits that engaging with these groups offers opportunities for liberation, combining faith with action to transformative change. In doing so, individuals participate in God's transformative work, much like Jesus's interactions with those on the margins shaped his ministry.

In this context, sainthood embodies virtues that facilitate a tie with God and others. As Eric Sammons describes in *Holiness for Everyone*, the Spanish priest Josemaría Escrivá (1902–75) and founder of *Opus Dei*, demonstrated that holiness can be accessible to ordinary people through practical, everyday spirituality. For Sammons, sainthood is not about achieving perfection but about continuous, intuitive, and creative growth that leads to genuine transformation. Escrivá's path draws richness from the margins, allowing saints to navigate diverse influences while remaining deeply connected to their spiritual core. This pilgrimage calls us to embrace diverse influences, advance a spirituality that upholds eternal authority, nurture a devoted relationship with God, encourage reflection, and drive toward moral action.

Diverse Traditions

Wholesome meals feed the body like mindful, spiritual practices that sustain the soul. Lumen Gentium highlights the universal call to holiness, inviting all believers to a pilgrimage of spiritual realization marked by openness to diverse traditions, humility, and communal support.[12]

The love of the Lord encompasses all people, emanating from his essence as the Creator of all. This supernatural love invites us to explore the multifaceted expressions of faith, much like savoring food's various tastes and textures. Just as family diets shape our familiarity with diverse flavors, our spiritual upbringing significantly influences how we experience and understand God's love. On this pilgrimage of spiritual growth, we are called to embrace the rich diversity of Christian traditions—like savoring different flavors in a well-prepared meal. Nourished by faith, this transformative pilgrimage adapts to the ever-changing world while strengthening a dynamic worldview.

Jesus's Jewish tradition had diverse perspectives on faith and spirituality. Scholars such as E. P. Sanders and Jacob Neusner have documented how distinct groups like the Sadducees, Pharisees, Essenes, and Zealots each held their worldviews and practices.[13] As Neusner emphasizes, the Pharisees focused on interpreting the oral law and integrating holiness into daily life. In contrast, the Sadducees, as described by Sanders, centered their customs around temple rituals and rejected the oral traditions upheld by the Pharisees.[14] The Essenes, as discussed extensively in Geza Vermes's work on the Dead Sea Scrolls, pursued a monastic, ascetic lifestyle, separating themselves from broader Jewish society.[15] Meanwhile, as depicted by Josephus, the Zealots championed political and military resistance against Roman rule, interpreting religious liberation as a call to national freedom.[16]

These diverse theological perspectives provide a framework for understanding the foundations of spiritual nourishment. Each group offers insights into critical aspects of spiritual growth. The Sadducees, focusing on upholding the law and maintaining religious authority, embody **Rectitude**, representing adherence to established principles and ethical integrity essential for a deep spiritual life. The Pharisees' emphasis on daily holiness parallels the building block of **Piety**, where devotion to God is consistently cultivated. The Essenes' commitment to spiritual purity through isolation mirrors the significance of **Solitude**, which creates space for introspection and mystical encounters that develop one's faith. Despite their political orientation, even the Zealots illustrate an aspect of **Rectitude**—the determination to stand firm in one's convictions.[17]

The diversity within Second Temple Judaism highlights faith's complexity and dynamic nature during that period. Just as these Jewish groups contributed to a rich and multifaceted religious environment, contemporary Christian spirituality thrives through various practices, beliefs, and theological interpretations. As Marcus Borg and John Dominic Crossan contend, maintaining a spirit of openness and curiosity to new spiritual insights unlocks transformative ways to encounter the sacred.[18]

Insights from the Margins

The most profound spiritual insights often come from those on the margins where hardship tests faith. Diverse and usually marginalized voices invite us to recognize that true spiritual richness arises not from status but faith, resilience, and grace—a richness that spans cultural, social, and economic backgrounds. Transcultural spirituality, like a chef blending flavors from diverse traditions, invites us to enrich our faith by incorporating diverse practices while staying grounded in Christ. These perspectives teach us humility, justice, and service, reminding us that sainthood lies not in perfection but in walking with others through their struggles. Authentic faith leads to a life of love, righteousness, and Christ's teachings. This approach resonates deeply with the Latine community, where *mestizaje*—blending Indigenous, European, and African traditions—is central to identity.[19] Drawing on Indigenous wisdom, African diaspora traditions, or Eastern Christian contemplative methods, we enrich our pilgrimage while keeping Christ at the center, nurturing a spirituality that cultivates our faith.[20]

Transcultural spirituality strengthens faith by emphasizing inner transformation rather than merely following religious practices. Actual spiritual growth reshapes the heart and character, allowing love, humility, and righteousness to flow naturally. Through spiritual disciplines and the guidance of the Holy Spirit, believers cultivate an authentic correlation with God that is lived out in daily life.

This concept resonates with the Latine experience, where inclusivity is central to cultural and spiritual identity. Latine spirituality is not static; it blends traditions, communities, and diverse influences, creating a deeply rooted and evolving faith. Just as transcultural spirituality bridges familiar and unfamiliar elements to draw people closer to God, Latine faith thrives on integrating different spiritual expressions, reinforcing a sense of belonging and godly union. In this way, transcultural spirituality nurtures personal transformation and strengthens faith by making it more inclusive, adaptive, and intensely lived.

Jesus's ministry embodied this openness, crossing cultural boundaries while remaining true to God's love. The Latine tradition of *mestizaje* demonstrates that vibrant spirituality embraces diversity while maintaining core principles. Incorporating insights from various traditions strengthens our spirituality, like adding global flavors to a cherished meal. This openness does not dilute our faith but enhances it. Incorporating diverse spiritual insights makes our faith more inclusive, dynamic, and resilient.

Liberation theology, as presented in *Mysterium Liberationis*, aligns with the transformative nature of transcultural spirituality by prioritizing faith as a lived experience of justice, solidarity, and inclusivity. Just as transcultural spirituality seeks inner transformation, liberation theology calls for a conversion of the heart that leads believers to embrace the marginalized and live out their faith in action. In the Latine experience, faith is inherently dynamic—blending cultural traditions, communal practices, and diverse spiritual expressions. This reinforces its theology by emphasizing that authentic faith is not confined to rigid doctrines but flourishes in contextual, evolving, and inclusive ways. Bridging theological reflection with social engagement, liberation theology, and transcultural spirituality strengthens faith, making it substantially transformative, inclusive, and rooted in the lived realities of diverse communities.

Box 1.1 ***Mysterium Liberationis*****: A Landmark in Liberation Theology**

This comprehensive, multiauthor theological work presents liberation theology's key themes, history, and methods. Edited by Jesuit theologians Ellacuría and Sobrino, it is an introduction and an advanced exploration of liberationist thought within Latin American struggles for justice.

Key Themes and Contributions

- **Historical Context**—Traces the emergence of liberation theology in response to poverty, oppression, and colonial legacies in Latin America.
- **Theological Foundations**—Examines the interplay between faith and social justice, drawing from Scripture and Catholic social teaching.
- **Methodology**—Advocates for a praxis-based approach, emphasizing action, reflection, and commitment to the marginalized.
- **Christology and Ecclesiology**—Reinterprets Jesus's mission in solidarity with the poor and critiques institutional structures that sustain inequality.
- **Martyrdom and Witness**—Highlights the sacrifices of theologians, clergy, and lay leaders, including Óscar Romero and Ellacuría.

Why It Matters

- It remains a **foundational text** for scholars, theologians, and activists in liberationist and contextual theologies.
- The book **challenged dominant theological paradigms**, placing the concerns of the poor at the center of Christian reflection.
- It **bridged academic and grassroots movements**, influencing pastoral work, political theology, and interfaith dialogues worldwide.

Legacy and Impact

Despite resistance from some within the Catholic Church, the themes inspire movements advocating for **human rights**, **economic justice**, and **Indigenous rights**. It stands as a testament to the enduring relevance of **liberation theology in the twenty-first century.**

(Ellacuría, Ignacio, and Jon Sobrino, eds. *Mysterium Liberationis: Fundamental Concepts of Liberation Theology*. Orbis Books, 1993.)

As we have discussed, spiritual fulfillment is accessible to all and enriched by multiple influences. The Latine experience shows that faith is dynamic, blending traditions like devotion to the Virgin of Guadalupe with Indigenous wisdom. **MPSR** provides the foundation, while transcultural spirituality adds richness, turning our spiritual lives into a nourishing feast for the soul.[21]

Creating a Spiritual Diet

Saints realize that the timing and rhythm of their spiritual approaches affect their depth and impact as well as their gradual transformation. These four virtues are chosen because they encapsulate an essential role in spiritual growth: **Majesty** amplifies reverence, **Piety** introduces warmth and devotion, **Solitude** enhances clarity and introspection, and **Rectitude** transforms and fortifies integrity. Together, they form the fundamental building blocks that impact all aspects of spiritual life, from personal devotion to communal interaction. I have learned that spirituality is like a finely tuned dish—each virtue enhances the whole and refines what we cultivate to the soul. As taste and smell guide a cook, spiritual intuition—trusting in the Holy Spirit and personal discernment—guides the spiritual pilgrimage. **Majesty** amplifies reverence, **Piety** brings warmth, **Solitude** offers clarity, and **Rectitude** grounds with integrity. Their dynamic interplay shapes the depth and richness of one's spiritual life.

Saints delicately use these virtues of **MPSR** to enrich a spiritually "alive" practice marked by intentional harmony. Lacking any single element skews this interplay, while overemphasis disrupts it: Without **Solitude**, clarity fades; missing **Majesty** weakens depth; ignoring **Piety** dulls warmth; and neglecting **Rectitude** compromises integrity. Conversely, too much **Majesty** can breed detachment, just as excessive **Solitude** may isolate rather than enlighten. Each virtue must remain in proportion, supporting the others to create a cohesive and life-giving spirituality. Also, saints thoughtfully select spiritual tools and techniques to sustain them through challenges and inspire growth, integrating the four virtues into every aspect of their pilgrimage. Guided by reflective cues rather than fixed routines, they maintain openness and curiosity, finding creativity and enjoyment in their faith. Nosrat's advice to cooks is to learn from successes and mistakes. This adaptable approach nurtures a dynamic spirituality shaped by resilience and joyful exploration.

Solidarity as a Practice of Building Blocks

When we reflect on the core virtues of **MPSR**, the Latine concept of solidarity—the bridge between theological reflection and praxis—offers a powerful reminder that our spirituality must go beyond inner cultivation to serve those in need. Latine theologians emphasize that theology becomes authentic and transformative through solidarity when our beliefs are embodied in empathy, compassion, and service.

- **Majesty** amplifies reverence, elevating our awareness of the eternal and facilitating a greater sense of awe in God's presence. This reverence drives us to see others as beloved Creations of God, thus inspiring solidarity as an expression of respect for God's Creation. **Majesty**'s strength lies in cultivating our sense of the sacred; however, it risks overshadowing other virtues if it becomes detached from action, forgetting that reverence must also draw us into relationships with others.
- **Piety** infuses warmth and devotion into our spiritual lives, adding depth through acts of love and association. As a "warmth-bringer," **Piety** enriches our spiritual life by grounding us in daily acts of faith. Through solidarity, **Piety** is expressed in personal devotion and acts of service that ripple out to benefit others. When practiced, **Piety** moves beyond personal spirituality into communal engagement, preventing it from becoming performative and instead nurturing genuine compassion.
- **Solitude** brings clarity and helps us reflect on how we can engage in just and ethical relationships. This time of reflection should guide us to act in ways that positively impact those around us and uphold justice in our interactions. It gives us space for introspection and discernment, allowing us to recognize how we are called to act. Latine theology reminds us that theological reflection gains power when translated into practice; **Solitude** helps us contemplate the needs of others and renew our commitment to serve. However, if overemphasized, **Solitude** can lead to detachment, leaving insights unacted upon rather than creating meaningful ties through solidarity.

- **Rectitude** transforms through integrity and moral grounding, guiding our actions toward justice. In solidarity, **Rectitude** becomes a force for social transformation, as ethical living calls us to advocate for individuals from marginalized backgrounds and act with integrity. While **Rectitude** provides a moral foundation across all practices, it must remain adaptable and compassionate. Overly rigid **Rectitude** risks moralism; it reflects a commitment to justice that is compassionate, not judgmental.

For liberation theology, when we unite these virtues with the call to solidarity, we see that each element of spiritual life gains more robust expression when oriented toward serving others. Then for *misión integral*, the gospel is most alive when love, justice, and faith intersect in acts of empathy and service, leading us to live out our beliefs as transformative expressions of the supernatural.

Virtues play a role in spiritual life, as salt, fat, acid, and heat form the basis of successful cooking. **MPSRs** are, similarly, essential pillars of a deep, resilient faith. Rather than following a rigid "recipe," saints learn to flexibly apply these elements—adapting them to life's varying stages—to embody Christ better and nurture curiosity toward God and diverse perspectives. Practically, this involves experimenting with each virtue, observing its impact, and gradually blending them. Over time, saints gain the confidence and skill to rely on the Holy Spirit for guidance, approaching a creative, resourceful spiritual life rather than a strict adherence to orthodoxy.

Saints can approach spirituality with greater confidence and authenticity by grasping how these virtues shape one's pilgrimage. Like adjusting flavors in cooking, spiritual growth demands continual reflection and aligning beliefs with actions to keep faith dynamic and responsive. Once grounded in these virtues, believers may explore new expressions of faith, much as Nosrat encourages cooks to experiment with ingredients and techniques. This approach nurtures flexibility and creativity, enabling individuals to adapt spiritual practices to their contexts while trusting their inner purpose. Freed from rigid rules, they cultivate a meaningful, context-sensitive faith that resonates deeply with their lives. Also, by focusing on a "spiritual diet," saints can embrace adaptability, enjoyment, and freedom in their interplay, like chefs applying universal cooking principles across diverse cuisines. These four virtues offer a foundational framework that transcends tradition or practice, supporting a holiness in every context. Inspired by Nosrat's vision, where cooking becomes an art of interplaying, this approach transforms faith into a nourishing and dynamic process. Emphasizing intuition, creativity, and introspection, it challenges believers to adapt their expressions of faith to their unique contexts while remaining rooted in these essential elements.

As you review this recipe, reflect on the four virtues and consider practical steps for incorporating them into your daily life. Only by intentionally integrating these elements can you develop a vibrant spiritual "diet" that nourishes your soul and enriches your community.

Chapter Two

Eat Your Kale and Also Your Avocado

Tradition is the living faith of the dead; traditionalism is the dead faith of the living.

—Jaroslav Pelikan

In *Orthodoxy*, G. K. Chesterton describes tradition as the "democracy of the dead," arguing that wisdom is not limited to the living but inherited from past generations. While democracy values every individual's voice, tradition extends this principle by respecting the insights of those who came before, challenging the tendency of modern thought to dismiss ancestral wisdom. Ellacuría's "historical reality" concept suggests spiritual nourishment involves personal growth and societal engagement.[1] The saint stands at the intersection of these two perspectives, embodying the bridge between the past and present. The saint finds meaning by drawing from the richness of tradition and actively engaging with the realities of the present.

As exemplified by saints' lives, spiritual practices should enrich us individually and benefit our communities. Saints integrate inherited wisdom with present-day experiences, much like a diet that requires various ingredients for nourishment. Chesterton critiques modern thought for ignoring the past, but the saint recognizes the importance of ancient wisdom in informing our spiritual lives today. Growth requires a blend of tradition and new experiences—just as a healthy diet requires old and new ingredients.

This chapter highlights the timeless virtues of **MPSR**, virtues passed down through the lives of saints. Yet it also emphasizes the saint's role in adapting these virtues to meet the challenges of today's context with cultural humility, creating a dynamic spiritual life that draws from both the wisdom of the past and the needs of the present in mutual interdependence.

The rich history of spiritual techniques—blending Catholic, Evangelical, Latin American, and Indigenous influences—forms the base of a Latine theology. Just as culinary traditions evolve through our own experiences, spiritual practices can be curated and modified by combining past wisdom with modern insight. To flesh out this dynamic, hear the *cuento* of Gorg the Giant, who was forced to learn vulnerability and openness to others' wisdom.

The Tale

Once upon a time, a village was filled with fear because a giant named Gorg lived nearby.[2] However, a curious boy named Juan wanted to discover the truth about him. When Juan found him, he was surprised to be greeted with warmth. The two spent time together, and Juan realized Gorg was not the monster people thought. When the villagers learned of their friendship, fear drove them to try to capture the giant.

Juan stood up for his friend, urging the villagers to see the kindness within the giant. Gorg's story teaches us that understanding often comes from unexpected places. Spiritual practices that seem foreign may initially seem uncomfortable, but they can nourish us, just as trying a new food can provide unexpected nourishment. Like Gorg, who embraced vulnerability, let us open our hearts to the wisdom of tradition and the gift of new paths, for only then does the spirit truly flourish.

Spiritual Nourishment in Diversity

Spiritual nourishment in diversity comes through articulating beliefs, integrating them into daily life, and collaborating in the community. As I have argued, spiritual fulfillment is a way of life (diet) available to all, and the core virtues of **MPSR** serve as essential spiritual superfoods, each nourishing and strengthening our relationship with God in unique and vital ways. I was reminded of this when my doctor pointed out that my diet, while rich in traditional foods, lacked the diversity of nutrients needed for optimal health. He recommended I incorporate new ingredients—like kale and avocado—to build a more robust, healthy lifestyle. Just as my physical health needs these nutrient-rich foods to thrive, our spiritual lives need these core virtues to grow strong and resilient. Particularly for those whose experiences differ from societal norms, these theological foundations of practical spiritual wholeness call for thoughtful articulation, integration, and collaborative inclusivity to honor each person's unique pilgrimage.

To cultivate spiritual health, we must master articulation, integration, and collaboration—bringing core virtues into the fabric of our daily lives and transforming abstract faith into lived, practical action. Chesterton's view on tradition shows that honoring the past need not limit growth but can guide our present. Like a varied diet, spiritual growth thrives on openness to new experiences while staying grounded in ancestral wisdom. Just as Gorg's richness was misunderstood until approached with curiosity, what seems unfamiliar in our spiritual pilgrimage can be vital for our growth when we embrace it with imagination. Where imagination fuels articulation, creativity guides integration and collaboration, and a nourishing and ever-renewing spirit grows.

Just as relying solely on kale can create a nutritional imbalance, overemphasizing one spiritual practice can hinder our overall growth. A healthy spiritual life, like a diet, thrives on variety. While tradition offers valuable wisdom, we must remain open to new habits to realize spiritual growth fully. Adding fresh insights to ancestral wisdom, like combining avocado with kale, results in a richer, more complete experience. Spiritual forms, like spices in a dish, contribute unique flavors to enrich our souls. Walter Brueggemann's concept of prophetic imagination encourages us to see new possibilities in our spiritual pilgrimage, reimagining the world from God's perspective. Similarly, Gorg's story teaches that what seems foreign can become a vital source of nourishment when approached with curiosity.

A nourished spiritual life requires the harmony of diverse practices. **Majesty** inspires awe for God's greatness, while **Piety** adds the warmth of love,

Box 2.1 Spiritual Nourishment in Diversity

Articulation expresses these principles in everyday actions.
Integration means blending them into daily life.
Collaboration emphasizes the importance of community.

creating a real relationship of reverence and devotion. **Solitude** allows us to reflect and absorb, but without **Rectitude**—ethical action—it risks becoming mere withdrawal. Each element enriches our walk like a well-prepared dish, helping us envision new possibilities for a vibrant, holistic spirituality.

These spiritual core virtues hold special relevance in Latine theologies, embodying the richness and diversity of faith traditions within these and other culturally varied communities. These theologies emphasize the integration of *lo cotidiano*—everyday lived experiences—with faith, embodying reverence for God's **Majesty** and a deep sense of **Piety** rooted in personal and communal devotion. **Solitude**, often found in moments of reflection within nature or silence, is paired with **Rectitude**, which requires active engagement in pursuing *la lucha* for justice and ethical living,[3] aligning with the central tenets of robustness. Brueggemann's prophetic imagination strongly resonates within these theologies, as it calls for envisioning a new world where faith actively engages with the social, political, and cultural realities of marginalized communities. Blending tradition with fresh perspectives, Latine theologies embody a spiritual "diet" nourishing the soul and the community through integration, justice, and relational depth.

Globally, in our spiritual diet, Lesslie Newbigin suggests that the gospel must be lived authentically daily in a diverse world.[4] We must integrate virtues from our already ordinary actions, allowing spirituality to infuse the routine and the struggle with the extraordinary. With the creativity of imagination, we adjust our spiritual practices as needed, balancing **Solitude** and community, tradition and innovation. The goal is wholeness with cultural humility, not perfection—a life that finds depth in daily experiences and flourishes through spiritual exploration, supported by our community for interdependence.

The Importance of Collaboration in Spiritual Nourishment

Chesterton tells us to honor tradition, and Gutiérrez encourages us to innovate so we do not get stuck in old ways. To truly grow, we need the wisdom of tradition and the willingness to adapt—like adding new ingredients to an old family recipe to make it even more vibrant and nourishing. Gutiérrez discusses liberation as freedom from oppression and a pilgrimage toward human flourishing.[5] With this, spiritual practices must intersect with solidarity and conscientization. However, saints also show us how to live rooted in tradition while being open to change. In *We Drink from Our Own Wells*, Gutiérrez reminds us that spiritual wholeness is not about fame or recognition but about drawing from our inner strength to live for God and the community.[6]

Table 2.1 The Core Ingredients and the Three Essential Implementations

Essential Implementations	Majesty	Piety	Solitude	Rectitude
Articulation Clearly expressing God's truth in our lives, sharing our faith, and being intentional with our spiritual expressions.	Articulation reflects **Majesty** by expressing God's truth with authority and clarity, revealing his grandeur.	Articulation honors **Piety** by articulating devotion through prayer, Scripture, and proclamation of faith.	Articulation in **Solitude** allows for deep reflection and private communication of God's truth.	Articulation embodies **Rectitude** by clearly speaking and living out truth, righteousness, and justice.
Integration Blending our spiritual practices into our daily lives, making faith a constant rhythm rather than an occasional activity.	Integration of spiritual practices into daily life showcases **Majesty** by embodying God's sovereignty in all aspects of life.	Integration aligns with **Piety** by blending spiritual discipline and devotion in daily actions.	Integration of **Solitude** and reflection strengthens one's personal relationship with God, balancing action with contemplation.	Integration of spiritual integrity and moral values ensures that daily actions reflect **Rectitude.**
Collaboration Working with others in community, just as ingredients harmonize a recipe. Saints do not walk the path alone, and neither do we.	Collaboration displays **Majesty** by honoring God's reign through united efforts in faith and community.	Collaboration reveals **Piety** in collective devotion, shared worship, and mutual support in faith communities.	Collaboration in **Solitude** can take the form of mutual encouragement for personal retreats and spiritual growth.	Collaboration in **Rectitude** involves strengthening justice and relational righteousness within community relationships and actions.

There is tension from going from within to outside ourselves and choosing these modes thoughtfully by sustaining ourselves, like having to select kale and avocado to improve my life and those around me. Spiritual practices must blossom and change yet hold on to their essence.

Kale and Avocado

Imagination and creativity are the kale and avocado of our spiritual lives, supporting cultural humility and mutual interdependence. Tradition anchors our faith, while innovation and creativity elevate our engagement, facilitating a spirit of shared growth and dynamic belief. As with a well-crafted meal that blends diverse ingredients into a cohesive whole, our spiritual "diet" becomes more satisfying when we integrate various rites and traditions, each contributing a distinct "flavor." Hispanic and Latin cuisine vividly illustrates this principle: Tamales—lovingly wrapped and steamed—symbolize familial unity and intergenerational heritage; ceviche, transformed by the tartness of lime, mirrors how life's challenging moments can refresh and renew; and mole, meticulously created from many ingredients over time, embodies the profound richness that emerges from patient, soulful preparation.[7] *Tamales*, rooted in Mesoamerican civilizations, continue to mark communal occasions; the citrus-based preparation of *ceviche*, originating on Peru's Pacific coast, highlights its transformative nature; and *mole*—with regional Mexican variations such as mole poblano—showcases the complex layering of heritage and celebration in Mexican cuisine. This suggests that such dishes also reflect cultural hybridity, where Indigenous and colonial influences blend to form something distinctive. Each culinary expression reinforces that faith and cuisine derive depth from time, care, and a willingness to explore new possibilities.

In the same way, in the sacred celebrations in Latine traditions, sainthood is not about individual perfection but about collective participation in the sanctified.[8] Latin American spiritual traditions, often expressed through communal rituals like Día de Muertos, emphasize the ancestors, the sacred, and everyday life. This perspective broadens the concept of sainthood, highlighting its collective, celebratory, and relational nature. Spiritual growth is an individual pursuit and a shared, joyful experience that strengthens personal and community bonds, affirming that the sacred and the mundane are intertwined. These celebrations, filled with offerings, prayers, and remembrances, cultivate a sense of continuity between the living and the dead, the present and the eternal. By incorporating such traditions into our spiritual diet, we cultivate our way to God, our ancestors, and the sacredness of life. The diet for spiritual fulfillment is accessible to all willing to follow it. Embodying God's core virtues is like having only the ingredients for a meal—each one essential but incomplete on its own.

In Latine culture, communal meals are more than sustenance—they are celebrations of life, family, and faith. Whether at religious events or family gatherings, these shared experiences encourage a connected sense of community and collective growth. Like spiritual practices, meals symbolize nourishment, love, and devotion, reflecting the intertwined nature of food and faith in Latin American traditions. This is communal spirituality: shared practices cultivating personal and collective faith, advancing engagement, support, and richer spiritual nourishment.[9] This is missional life, as Darrell Guder explains.[10] Saints, past and present, did not walk their pilgrimage alone. They worked alongside fellow believers, allowing their communities and spiritual traditions to shape their lives. Relying solely on one form, like eating only kale, risks spiritual malnourishment—fatigue, discouragement, and stagnation. Collaboration with others and drawing on the richness of multiple traditions sustain a holistic faith, preparing us for the Holy Feast in Revelation 5, where the fullness of God's table unites every nation in shared, eternal nourishment.[11]

Collaborating Spiritual Practices across Traditions

Think of collaboration as essential to both culinary and spiritual endeavors. A delicious recipe requires harmony and variety. In the same way, spiritual growth flourishes when we collaborate with others. Throughout history, saints have shown us the importance of working within faith communities, drawing on traditions and the strengths of others to cultivate collective growth. Saints were not lone champions of integrity, isolated in their pursuit of holiness.[12] They allowed their spiritual pilgrimages to be shaped by their communities, mentors, and the rich traditions they encountered. As we walk this path, we are also called to engage with others, learn from their wisdom, and allow the broader supportive spiritual community to shape our spiritual practices. Collaboration helps us transcend individual limitations, bringing out the richness and depth of our spiritual lives.

Spiritual collaboration encompasses an intercultural exchange of expressions that enrich and nourish the soul. Across traditions—such as Catholicism, Protestantism, and Eastern Orthodoxy—a diverse array of spiritual practices offers valuable insights into a suitable communion with God. Integrating these varied ways cultivates a more holistic and spiritual life, combining complementary elements to create a comprehensive and robust foundation for spiritual growth. Our spirituality is fortified, not weakened, by embracing diverse traditions; like vital ingredients in a diet, each virtue is powerful alone but transformative.

Nourishment for the Soul

As diet impacts our physical and mental well-being, our spiritual practices affect the whole of who we are—our *nephesh* (נֶפֶשׁ), the Hebrew word for soul, which encompasses the entirety of our being.[13] In Psalm 23:3 (ESV), we read, "He restores my *nephesh*," often translated as "soul." Yet *nephesh* encompasses far more than just a spiritual element; it signifies the entirety of one's being—body, mind, and spirit united.[14] When we consider God restoring our *nephesh*, it is an invitation to see how the sacred care extends to every part of who we are. God is refreshing a part of us and rejuvenating our whole person. This holistic renewal reflects the fullness of life and vitality, grounding our spirituality in every aspect of our humanity. Through *nephesh*, the Bible thoroughly addresses us, drawing strength from God, who restores us, body and soul.[15] By applying spiritual principles through the lens of *nephesh*, a person nurtures holistic well-being, integrating these applications into daily life to care for both body and soul. Collaboration then—whether with individuals, communities, or spiritual practices—is a critical element of balancing all aspects of life, supporting the flourishing of the *nephesh* in its fullness.

Latine theologies emphasize the inseparability of spiritual, emotional, and physical well-being from the other. This concept is crucial to understanding the holistic nature of faith.[16] This understanding ultimately leads to the flourishing of the individual and the broader community, supporting a holistic spirituality deeply rooted in shared life. In the Latine context, this perspective resonates profoundly, as faith is actively lived in solidarity with others, intertwining spiritual practices with daily life. Here, spirituality is not an isolated pursuit but a collective pilgrimage, where the well-being of one enriches the whole community, embodying the *nephesh*-inspired commitment to care for the complete self within the fabric of communal existence.[17]

Our spiritual diets should nourish us comprehensively and sustainably to keep us connected to what God is already doing. *Missio Dei*, meaning "the mission of God," emphasizes that mission originates from God's nature and purpose rather than merely an activity of the church. Rooted in Karl Barth's theology, it envisions the church participating in God's work of redemption and reconciliation. Scholars like David J. Bosch traced its historical development, while Lesslie Newbigin explored its implications for a pluralistic world. Participation in the *missio Dei* calls saints to collaborate in this celestial mission, bringing nourishment, transformation, and restoration to their lives and the world around them.[18] As saints participate in the vocation, they bring God's mission to life through everyday actions, embodying the core virtues and values essential to a saintly life. The collaboration then is within individuals, traditions, and my *nephesh* but also with God's works to redeem and restore the world to its intended wholeness. This mission calls saints to be agents of God's love and compassion, bringing healing and hope to a broken world.

A spiritually nourishing life challenges saints to participate actively in God's mission, aligning their actions with God's purpose through a collective and dynamic approach.[19] This is viewed by Boff's understanding of the Holy Trinity as a model of community and mutual love that guides us to participate in the relational love of the Father, Son, and Holy Spirit.[20] This participation is the essence of sainthood: engaging in God's love, allowing it to flow through us, and reflecting it in our actions. To holistically address spiritual and physical needs, the *missio Dei* involves various elements—evangelism, social action, community care, and transformative grace. This mission is deep and layered, requiring saints to work together, developing growth, renewal, and transformation, individually and as a community, to bring about God's Kingdom on earth. As we partner in God's mission, we spread joy and peace, find purpose, and experience deep spiritual nourishment while interacting between the parts.

Ordinary Saints in Extraordinary Faith

Saints are not those striving for unattainable perfection but those who respond to God's vocation to join God "outside the city gate" (Heb. 13:12)—where grace, love, and justice flourish. This is where true holiness is found—not in institutions of power or places of privilege but at the margins, among people with lived experiences of marginalization and individuals from marginalized backgrounds, where Christ dwells. As Costas explores in *Christ Outside the Gate*, sainthood is lived beyond the boundaries of comfort and acceptance in places where God's redemptive work is most needed.[21] Sainthood is not about miraculous deeds or grand gestures but about faithfully embracing God's grace and allowing it to shape our thoughts, words, and actions as we stand in solidarity with those in need. This mission takes us outside the boundaries of comfort, challenging us to align our lives with God's will by engaging with those on the margins (for me, this is kale and avocado!).

Western and Eastern Christian traditions may offer different perspectives on sainthood—one often focused on individual **Piety**, the other on communal holiness. Like preparing kale and avocado in various ways to nourish the body, these traditions offer distinct yet complementary paths to holiness, reminding us that there is no single way to sainthood. It is about how we respond to God's grace in the unique circumstances of our lives as individuals and as communities. The lives of saints like Paul (Rom. 1:7) and Peter (1 Pet. 2:9) illustrate that sainthood is not reserved for a select few; it is within reach of anyone who seeks to align themselves with God's will. These saints were ordinary individuals who embodied God's love through humility, kindness, and compassion in standing with the people facing oppression and in their everyday interactions. True holiness is found "outside the gate," where love, grace, and service to others are lived out.

Sainthood is an invitation to participate in God's mission outside where Jesus died actively. It is not about being perfect or possessing extraordinary abilities; it is about living a life of faith rooted in God's grace, allowing that grace to flow through every part of our lives. Saints, past and present, remind us that this calling is accessible to all. Living in alignment with God's will and working for justice and love, we participate in God's mission and reflect God's presence in the world—transforming ourselves and our communities through extraordinary faith.

Crisis as a Catalyst for Spiritual Growth

Crises have the potential to become profound moments of spiritual transformation, much like how unexpected ingredients can change a recipe for the better. During times of crisis, we often find ourselves seeking new spiritual practices—adding "new ingredients" to our spiritual diet that nourish us in unexpected ways. These challenges force us to explore beyond our usual routines, adding depth, trust, patience, and resilience to our faith pilgrimage.[22]

The story of my friend's family in South America illustrates this vividly. A tragic snowmobile accident led to the discovery of a hidden brain tumor, revealing an unexpected blessing amid fear. This crisis brought a profound test of faith, forcing my friend's father to grapple with the complexities of trusting God through suffering. Yet through these challenges, the family discovered a deeper layer of God's grace—a grace that does not always fit neatly into our understanding but transforms us. The ordeal enriched their spiritual lives, like a diet enhanced by unexpected ingredients; cultivated their faith; and expanded their trust in God.

Crises are like the heat and pressure transforming a dish—revealing new dimensions of our faith and forcing us to confront our beliefs and assumptions. Just as theologians like Gutiérrez and Costas remind us that transformation happens in community and love, our spiritual pilgrimage is enriched by embracing new experiences and challenges. Our spiritual diet must incorporate variety and the willingness to be reshaped by God's grace. Sainthood is not about perfection but about being open to ongoing transformation—allowing crises to cultivate our faith and embracing the unexpected with trust and humility.

Revolutionary Spiritual Practices

Saints use what they have access to to cultivate this spiritual diet. In many cases, this is a revolution, which is the work of reshaping society with justice and love and bringing dignity to all in God's vision. Revolutionary spiritual practices push us to rethink the foundations of our spiritual growth, challenging us to move beyond the comfort of familiar routines and embrace new ways of engaging with the world.[23] Inspired by liberation theology and ideas from *Beyond Liberation Theology* by Humberto Belli,[24] this approach to spirituality mirrors the work of leaders like Chávez and Bartolomé de las Casas, who fought for justice in their respective contexts.[25] Just as Chávez took a stand against unjust labor in the grape fields and de las Casas fought for the rights of Indigenous peoples, our spiritual growth must be enriched by revolutionary actions that connect our faith to justice, solidarity, and advocacy.

Latin American revolutionary spiritual practices reveal resistance through acts of love, merging faith with the struggle for justice and dignity. In the face of oppression, poetry and murals have become sacred expressions of resilience, channeling the hopes and voices of marginalized communities. For example, Pablo Neruda's poems and Diego Rivera's murals are not merely art but revolutionary acts of love. Neruda's verses often celebrate the ordinary people, championing their dignity and struggles, while Rivera's murals portray the lives of workers and Indigenous peoples, affirming their value and resilience. These creative forms become spiritual acts of resistance, speaking truth to power and bolstering solidarity. In this way, cultural hybridity transforms art into a means of resistance, where love defies oppression and lifts the humanity of all.

These practices are not about adhering to a rigid formula but about integrating diverse spiritual disciplines that are responsive to the realities of our world. For example, *mujerista*, as a revolutionary method, encourages integrating faith with the struggle for social justice, emphasizing solidarity, mutual support, and collective liberation from the mothers, daughters, and grandmothers in their contexts.[26] True spirituality is contextual—it thrives when rooted in the pursuit of justice, recognizing cultural diversity, and participating in God's mission. Liberation theology teaches us that spirituality must engage with justice, context, and cultural issues.[27] A vibrant spiritual life requires equilibrium, introducing diverse disciplines that nourish our faith pilgrimage in holistic and transformative ways. In this way, Latin American spirituality transforms art into a means of resistance, where love defies oppression and sustains our spirit through diversity and renewal.

Drawing from the insights of theologians such as Támez, Boff, and Sobrino, revolutionary spiritual practices move us toward a deeper, more engaged sainthood. Támez's theology reminds us that spirituality must address gender and oppression,[28] while Boff's ecological theology shows that spiritual growth is intertwined with the earth's health.[29] Sobrino's Christology invites us to see Christ in marginalized individuals and respond to their suffering with compassion and action.[30] These perspectives challenge us to integrate justice, Creation care, and solidarity into our spiritual traditions, ensuring they remain relevant, adaptable, and aligned with God's will with imagination and creativity.

Some have given their lives in these revolutions, yet through their sacrifice, they showed the greatest love. Revolutionary spiritual practices connect deeply with the core virtues of **MPSR** with the methods of articulation, integration, and collaboration. **Majesty** aligns us with God's will, much like the focus on justice and liberation reflects God's concern for the people facing oppression. **Piety** is about recognizing God's presence in individuals from marginalized backgrounds and Creation, expanding devotion beyond personal reflection to include environmental stewardship. **Solitude** provides a reflective space to discern how issues like justice and ecology shape our faith—a moment for deep contemplation leads to growth. **Rectitude** emphasizes integrity and moral courage, urging us to reflect God's righteousness in confronting oppression and injustice. These revolutionary approaches challenge us to articulate, integrate, and collaborate in our faith pilgrimage, driving us to enact meaningful change in the world.

Liberation theology's revolutionary methods—conscientization, nonviolent resistance, and liturgical celebration—serve as clear and practical avenues for articulating, integrating, and collaborating. Conscientization, seen in Paulo Freire's literacy work in Brazil or the *comunidades eclesiales de base*, articulates the ingrained injustices that shape the lives of marginalized communities while sustaining critical awareness that leads to action.[31] This critical awareness is easily integrated into the lived experience of people facing oppression groups through relatable, participatory frameworks like Bible studies or community discussions.[32] Nonviolent resistance, exemplified by Óscar Romero's advocacy for soldiers to refuse unjust orders or the peaceful protests of the Mothers of the Plaza de Mayo, integrates spiritual and ethical values into a response to injustice, offering a model for collective action that can be widely embraced across diverse communities.[33] These forms of resistance articulate the moral responsibility to confront oppression without perpetuating violence, encouraging collaboration across different sectors of society—including churches, human rights groups, and grassroots organizations—to stand together for justice.[34] Liturgical celebrations, such as the *misa campesina* or stations of the cross processions in El Salvador, symbolize and embody the people's struggles, providing a space to integrate faith with action. Through the language, rituals, and symbols that resonate with local cultures, these celebrations uphold collaboration by uniting communities in shared expressions of trust and solidarity.[35]

Together, these practices articulate the vision of a just society, integrate transformative action into the faith experience, and encourage collaboration for systemic change. These revolutionary practices move us to communicate our faith through actions that address social and environmental challenges. They integrate justice, Creation care, and solidarity with individuals from marginalized backgrounds into every part of our spiritual pilgrimage, making our faith a lived reality. We are called to participate in God's redemptive work, embodying a revolutionary spirituality by transforming ourselves and our communities.

Integration of Praxis with Community

Saints must methodically plan their diets with implementation, articulation, and collaboration across Christian traditions to cultivate a spiritually nourishing life. Through revolutionary spiritual actions, saints expand their spiritual "diet" and experience God in transformative ways. Using these practices in everyday life helps maintain a dynamic and relevant faith—through community engagement and shared learning—further strengthens faith by drawing on collective wisdom. This approach to spiritual formation aligns the lives of saints with God's will, ensuring that their spirituality remains adaptive, rich, and responsive to the world's needs.

Spiritual practices from different perspectives connect deeply to heritage, community, and legacy. These traditions add richness and depth to our spiritual lives, akin to adding vibrant new ingredients to a simple meal. Saints are encouraged to embrace new spiritual practices, ensuring their pilgrimage remains vibrant, dynamic, and fulfilling. Approaching these new ways with curiosity and openness allows saints to broaden their spiritual "palate." Not every behavior will resonate with everyone, but embracing diversity ensures robust spiritual growth and helps build relationships with God and others. Overcoming fear of the unfamiliar, saints create stability and enrich the life of faith, making it adaptable to changing needs. A spiritually nourishing life requires articulation, integration, and collaboration. These principles allow saints to cultivate a rich spiritual diet and align with God's mission.

Connecting reflection with action promotes spiritual growth that impacts individuals and society. Spiritual engagement must advance God's justice, cultivating inner transformation and social impact. Saints do not walk this path alone; they flourish by participating in God's mission within their community, recognizing the importance of relationships and shared purpose. The blending of influences from different traditions shapes spiritual growth, allowing saints to thrive in the presence of community and collaboration. Walking alongside others is central to spiritual growth. Saints must nurture relationships that lead to mutual growth, shared purpose, and healing. Community-centered spirituality teaches us that spiritual growth is not an individual endeavor but a communal pilgrimage enriched by others' contributions and the diversity of others.

Articulating, integrating, and collaborating across traditions allows saints to create a life aligned with God's mission. Mission and spirituality must be culturally integrated, reflecting the diverse realities of the world. Saints must develop a holistic faith that draws from different traditions, creating a spiritual pilgrimage that is adaptable, resilient, and connected to God's purpose. Faith, like food, is more fulfilling when shared. Community allows saints to habituate humility, compassion, and patience, growing together in faith and commitment to God's mission. The wise saint steps beyond the familiar through articulation, integration, and collaboration, embracing diverse practices and new growth paths.

Spiritual growth is enriched by a diverse spiritual diet that brings together different behaviors and perspectives. Incorporating the richness of diverse traditions into our spiritual lives, saints cultivate a dynamic faith that is deeply connected to God and the community. A spiritually nourishing life involves integrating diverse processes, articulating God's truth, and collaborating with others in the community. Saints are called to embrace new spiritual practices—rooted in tradition yet open to innovation—creating a dynamic spiritual pilgrimage. Through shared experiences, openness, and commitment to God's calling, individuals embody love and grace in their communal lives.

God's mission moves saints to participate in God's transformative work. This involves nourishing themselves and those around them. Through collaboration, openness, and a commitment to a diverse spiritual diet, saints cultivate a rich, adaptive, and dynamic faith life. This participation requires embracing new systems and stepping outside of comfort zones. Saints are not meant to live in isolation, relying solely on familiar traditions; they must diversify their spiritual practices, continually seeking to grow and adapt to the world's challenges. In this way, they nourish themselves and their communities, embracing justice, liberation, and solidarity principles.

The transformative potential of sainthood emerges from uniting traditional orthodoxy with innovative practices, drawing upon historical insight while embracing contemporary perspectives for today's spiritual journey. Saints are encouraged to adopt an "outside the gate" mindset, engaging deeply with others and embodying God's grace in demanding contexts. Like enriching a meal with kale and avocado, this "transformative diet" underscores how stability in tradition can be invigorated by revolutionary acts of justice and compassion.

Table 2.2 The Three Essential Implementations

Implementations	Definition	Biblical Example	Latine Example	MPSR
Articulation	Expressing God's truth clearly and authentically in word and action.	Paul's letters articulate Christian doctrine (Romans, Corinthians).	Hispanic storytelling and oral traditions conveying spiritual truths.	Articulation reflects **Majesty** by proclaiming God's truth with authority.
Integration	Harmonizing spiritual practices with daily life in work, family, and worship.	Jesus's integration of prayer and action in daily ministry (Luke 5:16).	Blending Indigenous, Catholic, and local traditions (Día de Muertos).	Integration aligns with **Piety** by living a life devoted to spiritual practices.
Collaboration	Working with others in faith and growing in community.	The early Christian community sharing all things in common (Acts 2:44).	Communal meals and processions (*Las Posadas*, communal prayers).	Collaboration embodies **Rectitude** by building righteous community relationships.

Participation in the *missio Dei* entails active involvement in Christ's work of redemption and restoration, often requiring individuals to step beyond familiar comforts. Guided by the Holy Spirit, growth unfolds through discomfort and crisis, wherein unfamiliar territory becomes a source of renewal. Spiritual development relies on articulation, integration, and collaboration—virtues embodied by MPSR—that flourish within a diversified spiritual "diet." Sainthood is communal: Shared hardship, radical openness, and transcending boundaries advance personal and collective flourishing in a united journey toward deeper faith and renewed hope.

Part Two

The Building Blocks

So you say you love the poor . . . name them.

—Gustavo Gutiérrez

Chapter Three

Exploring the Spiritual Building Blocks

A theology which has as its points of reference only "truths" which have been established once and for all—and not the Truth which is also the Way—can only be static and, in the long run, sterile.

—Gustavo Gutiérrez

True spirituality isn't just about personal growth—it is also about making a difference in the world. It is an interplay between cultivating your spirituality and putting it into action. It is not just about what you know or feel; it is about bringing your heart and mind into the pilgrimage. This idea isn't new—it has been a core part of Christian and Jewish traditions for centuries. Thinkers like Gutiérrez and Romero have reinforced the idea that genuine faith isn't just personal; it is meant to create change. When spirituality is lived out this way, it becomes fulfilling and a force for good in the world.

Four essential theological foundations—**MPSR**—create a dynamic and transformative framework in the spiritual pilgrimage, much like the core ingredients of a well-crafted recipe. These elements form the foundation for a holistic and aligned approach to spiritual growth, guiding believers through cognitive, emotional, transcendent, and immanent experiences and nourishing the soul in a way that honors God.

As Gutiérrez wisely stated, "A theology which has as its points of reference only 'truths' which have been established once and for all—and not the Truth which is also the Way—can only be static and in the long run sterile." His words illuminate the need for a flexible and evolving theology that embraces the richness of human experience, culture, and relationships. In the same way, the ingredients of a spiritual life must complement and enhance one another, forming an adaptable yet grounded faith.

- **Majesty** is the salt, enhancing every other practice by grounding us in God's Sacred Authority and purpose.
- **Piety** is the fat, enriching our faith through devotion, prayer, and service, adding depth and warmth.
- **Solitude** is the acid that sharpens our spiritual clarity by cutting through distractions and bringing fresh insight.
- **Rectitude** is the heat, binding everything with integrity and discipline, fortifying our actions.

As depicted in the diagram in Figure 3.1, these building blocks span different aspects of our spiritual experience: cognitive and affective, transcendent and immanent. **Majesty** and **Rectitude** guide our understanding and actions, while **Piety** and **Solitude** cultivate our emotional and spiritual correlation. Together, these elements create a nourishing spiritual "diet" that integrates the intellectual pursuit of faith and the emotional experience.

Using Urban T. Holmes III's analytical tool,[1] the image of the quadrants provides a visual layout of these four blocks, illustrating how they interact across the axes of spiritual experience. **Majesty** (queen or king) is in the cognitive, *kataphatic* quadrant, representing leadership, governance, and the intellectual authority to lead with wisdom. **Rectitude** (warrior), by contrast, occupies the cognitive, *apophatic* quadrant, embodying ethical living and justice as transcendent ideals that guide one's capacity to act with righteousness.

Piety (priest) finds its place in the affective, kataphatic quadrant on the emotional axis, reflecting the profoundly personal and immanent link to God through daily devotion and prayer. **Solitude** (mystic), in the affective, apophatic quadrant, calls for emotional vulnerability and retreat, offering a space for quiet reflection and bonding with God without distractions. When properly understood and integrated, these four blocks address the full spectrum of human experience, leading to a more robust and comprehensive spiritual life.

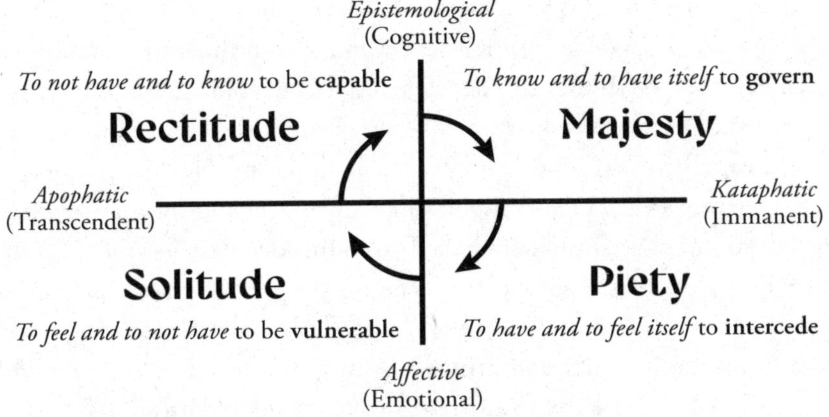

Figure 3.1 MPSR Defined by Quadrants

The Dynamic Framework for Spiritual Growth

For Holmes, the heart of the *Circle of Sensitivity* lies in expanding one's awareness and empathy to better understand and respond to the emotions and needs of others. This blended approach ensures that no single aspect of faith dominates at the expense of others. Focusing solely on governance and leadership (**Majesty**) without devotion (**Piety**) or justice (**Rectitude**) can lead to a detached spirituality. Similarly, a contemplative or devoted life (**Solitude** or **Piety**) without engagement in justice or leadership risks isolation and stagnation.

Harmonizing these four pillars, Latine spirituality becomes intellectually grounded and emotionally rich, ensuring it remains relevant and resilient in changing times. The four foundational principles form an integrated framework for spiritual formation that sustains dynamic engagement with the complexities of faith. Each principle contributes uniquely to developing the believer's intellectual, emotional, transcendent, and immanent capacities while allowing for flexibility and adaptation to varying contexts and times. As this chapter unfolds, these foundational principles will be examined in greater depth, demonstrating how their dynamic integration promotes spiritual flourishing. This flexible approach enables believers to cultivate wisdom, discipline, contemplation, and ethical living, equipping them to navigate the evolving challenges of faith in an ever-changing world.

For example, Nidia (a pseudonym used for this illustration) will exemplify a dynamic and adaptable spirituality, engaging with the four foundational principles in response to the unique demands of her context. **Majesty** guides her leadership within her community, where she provides vision and direction rooted in her belief in God's authority. She draws on **Piety** to maintain a disciplined devotional life, incorporating daily prayer and spiritual practices that sustain her faith amid her challenges. **Solitude** offers her the reflective space to process her experiences, leading to deeper spiritual insights that shape her understanding of God's work in her life. Finally, **Rectitude** grounds Nidia in ethical integrity and justice, ensuring that her actions align with her values, particularly in her advocacy for marginalized groups.

Rather than holding these principles in a static balance, Nidia demonstrates how they interact fluidly in response to the shifting needs of her life and context. When community leadership requires decisive action, she leans more heavily on **Majesty** and **Rectitude**, while in quieter seasons, she turns to **Solitude** and **Piety** to renew her spirit. Her spiritual practices evolve with the circumstances, illustrating how these principles adapt to the cultural, historical, and personal challenges she encounters.

Nidia's Spiritual Diet through MPSR

In the **MPSR** quadrants framework, Nidia's actions are real-world examples of how these blocks can manifest in someone's life. Figure 3.2 shows how these quadrants showcase these blocks interacting in Nidia's example of balancing one another, guiding personal growth, and impacting the community.

- **Majesty** *(epistemological, kataphatic)*: In the quadrant of **Majesty**, Nidia demonstrates leadership that stems from an enhanced sense of self, confident governance, and intellectual stimulation. She takes on leadership roles within her community, making informed decisions that inspire and guide others. This quadrant emphasizes how management and leadership, rooted in wisdom, can advance transformation in individual and communal contexts. **Majesty** enables Nidia to lead confidently while continually engaging in intellectual growth, ensuring her leadership is authoritative and evolving.

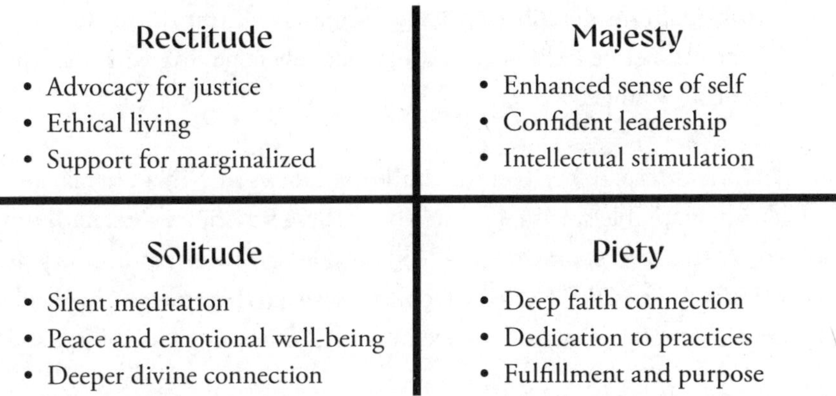

Figure 3.2 MPSR Quadrants of the Divine with Nidia's Example

- **Piety** *(affective, kataphatic)*: **Piety** embodies Nidia's link to her faith through daily devotional practices and rituals. She finds fulfillment and purpose in this quadrant, dedicating herself to spiritual discipline. Nidia's engagement with **Piety** shows how daily devotion creates a foundation for sustaining other spiritual virtues, ensuring faith remains active and deeply felt. **Piety** emphasizes the importance of dedication and intercession, grounding Nidia's leadership and justice work in her consistent relationship with God.
- **Solitude** *(affective, apophatic)*: In the **Solitude** quadrant, Nidia practices silent meditation and personal reflection, cultivating peace and emotional well-being. This personal reflection and retreat time allows her to develop her tie to God, helping her maintain clarity and focus. **Solitude** provides Nidia with the necessary emotional space to process the challenges of leadership and justice work, reminding her of the need for self-care and personal union with God in the quiet moments of her life.
- **Rectitude** *(epistemological, apophatic)*: Finally, **Rectitude** is where Nidia advocates for justice and ethical living. She supports marginalized communities and stands up for justice, ensuring her faith is personal and social. **Rectitude** requires her to align her actions with moral principles, fighting for what is right even when complicated.

This quadrant demonstrates how Nidia's faith transforms her into a force for justice in her community, actively engaging with the world to bring change.

The dynamic interplay between the building blocks in Nidia's life creates a flexible and adaptable spiritual framework. These principles interact fluidly, allowing Nidia to respond to the evolving needs of her community and personal life. They make a holistic (robust) spiritual diet, integrating leadership, devotion, reflection, and justice into a cohesive, impactful faith style.

Leadership in a Community Context

Majesty in Christian spirituality is not simply about authority or power but about leading with wisdom and a deep commitment to justice. Gutiérrez emphasizes that authentic spiritual leadership must be rooted in solidarity with the poor and marginalized. For Gutiérrez, leadership is not a distant exercise in governance but a humble service that actively engages in the struggles for justice. This reflects how **Majesty** operates in the spiritual realm, where leadership embodies Christ's commitment to the least of these.

Padilla and Escobar emphasize that faith leadership must involve a holistic mission, where proclaiming the gospel goes hand in hand with addressing social justice and poverty.[2] This understanding of **Majesty** aligns with the concept that proper spiritual authority comes from serving individuals from marginalized backgrounds and advocating for systemic change within communities. Their view of leadership as both proclamation and social action enriches the understanding of **Majesty** as eternal governance rooted in service and justice.

Similarly, Jon Sobrino reminds us that the crucified peoples of Latin America reflect Christ's suffering.[3] Thus, **Majesty** in leadership demands standing with the people facing oppression, even to the point of martyrdom, as exemplified by Romero. Romero's relationships transcended mere words; they represented a public, transformative force that spoke out against systemic injustice and called the church to live out its prophetic role in society.[4] In this sense, **Majesty** as a virtue is about leading with moral courage and authority while remaining grounded in community service and advocacy.

In faith leadership, **Majesty** is not merely an abstract trait or intellectual quality; it is an active and transformative force that empowers communities and individuals to flourish. **Majesty** in leadership embodies both the wisdom to govern and the grace to inspire others. Without it, spiritual practices may lack the direction and power to influence broader communities effectively. In the context of the **Majesty** quadrant, leadership is anchored in knowing and having—knowledge of principles and possession of authority to guide others toward a shared vision. This blend is essential for faith leaders who aim to cultivate transformation within themselves and in the broader supportive spiritual community.

Majesty occupies the kataphatic/cognitive quadrant, which focuses on governance and leadership that comes from understanding wisdom and applying it to everyday decision-making. In this quadrant, leadership is not simply about intellectual prowess; leadership is about embodying a sense of authority that reflects Christlike leadership. When faith leaders embrace this role, they move beyond mere knowledge into governing with grace, confidence, and humility.

In the Latine tradition, **Majesty** is often expressed through communal celebrations, processions, and shared rituals that symbolize collective leadership. These public acts of faith remind us that leadership is about not individual power but uplifting and inspiring communities. Boff's writings on communities' ecclesial base further support this notion, advocating for a profoundly spiritual and politically engaged church that reflects God's Kingdom on earth.[5] This form of **Majesty** brings forth transformative leadership that empowers believers to work together toward spiritual and societal renewal.[6]

Box 3.1 Ecclesial Base Communities

Rooted in liberation theology, ecclesial base communities are small Christian groups, often in marginalized areas, where laypeople engage in gospel reflection and social justice activism. Boff saw them as vital for spiritual growth and resistance to oppression. (Boff, Leonardo. *Ecclesiogenesis: The Base Communities Reinvent the Church*. Orbis Books, 1986.)

In Latine cultures, *fiestas religiosas* (religious festivals) and public processions serve as communal expressions of faith, reinforcing spiritual devotion and social bonds. Rooted in the Catholic tradition, these celebrations honor saints and the Virgin Mary, or significant religious events through masses, gatherings, and processions where believers carry icons and symbols of faith through the streets. Beyond rituals, they embody collective leadership and public witness, illustrating how **Majesty** manifests in action, bringing energy, visibility, and unity to the spiritual community. Leaders in these contexts do not operate in isolation but draw their authority from a collective wisdom that involves participation and shared responsibility.[7] For example, religious festivals in Latin America often involve entire communities, symbolizing unity and shared spiritual leadership.

This communal expression of **Majesty** reflects a broader understanding of leadership that transcends individual power. It offers modern faith leaders a powerful example of how to inspire and mobilize communities. Public processions and *fiestas religiosas* energize the supportive spiritual community, making the church's presence visible and accessible. These acts of devotion can be a transformative force in faith leadership today, helping to ground authority in a communal and participatory context and aligning well with the dynamic leadership required in multicultural and diverse societies.

The syncretism between Indigenous practices and colonial Catholicism often seen in Latin America demonstrates how spiritual authority can serve as a space for cultural resistance. Under colonial rule, many Indigenous communities adapted Christian symbols—such as images of saints or liturgical processions—to fit their customs and artistic expressions. This dynamic form of **Majesty**—a reverent leadership style blending Indigenous heritage with Catholic forms—enabled them to preserve cultural identity while navigating external pressures. Rather than surrendering to complete assimilation, Indigenous leaders turned Christian ceremonies into expressions of local artistry and communal values, safeguarding both tradition and spiritual governance in the face of colonial influence.

The Argument for Majesty as a Transformative Force

When fully embraced, **Majesty** allows Christians to take on leadership roles with intellectual understanding and authority. This form of leadership is not about control or domination; it is about guiding others toward spiritual transformation with wisdom, care, and communal engagement. The **Majesty** quadrant is essential for leaders who wish to influence their communities profoundly, ensuring that governance is grounded in knowledge and grace. Drawing from Latine communal leadership traditions, where collective decision-making and public spiritual expressions are commonplace, leaders can learn to stabilize intellectual authority with community-building practices. This combination enhances the leader's ability to govern and the community's sense of shared responsibility and unity. Leaders who understand the role of **Majesty** in this context do not just lead; they empower others to rise in their spiritual authority, creating a ripple effect of transformation that can profoundly impact the broader community. This form of leadership, rooted in individual insight and collective wisdom, embodies **Majesty** as a transformative force within communal spiritual life.

Modern faith leaders can infuse their communities with energy, purpose, and direction by integrating this dynamic form of leadership with the rich collective and public faith expression traditions. **Majesty** is, therefore, not only a personal quality but a communal one, acting as a catalyst for collective growth and transformation.

Devotion and Discipline in Daily Life

Piety, understood as the virtue of devotion and discipline, remains central to a vibrant, active spiritual life. In her feminist-liberation theology, Gebara reframes **Piety** by grounding it in the everyday realities of women, where prayer and daily tasks intertwine with the ongoing struggle for dignity and justice;[8] this expands **Piety** by grounding it in the lived experiences of Latine women, where prayer and daily devotion intertwine with the ongoing struggle for justice and dignity. In her framework, **Piety** emerges not as a distant ideal but as an everyday practice shaping how individuals work, care for family, and advocate for the marginalized. Similarly, Óscar Romero embodied **Piety** by linking faith to bold advocacy for marginalized communities, demonstrating that devotion can—and should—fuel the pursuit of social reform. He was assassinated while performing the most holy sacrament.[9]

Juan Sepúlveda's work in Pentecostalism expands the concept of **Piety** to include communal expressions of devotion, mainly through Spirit-led worship, prayer, and healing.[10] He argues that Pentecostal prayer practices are not solely individual acts but vital communal styles that nurture personal and communal faith. This approach to **Piety** reflects a holistic view where daily devotion and spiritual discipline bind believers to the Holy Spirit and one another, reinforcing spiritual growth through active and communal participation.

Boff also expands on this theme by incorporating ecological spirituality into the concept of **Piety**.[11] For Boff, devotion to God must include Creation care, highlighting that spiritual discipline cannot be separated from the world around us. This holistic view of **Piety**, which emphasizes the interconnectedness of all living things, calls believers to a daily reflection on God's love for humanity and the earth. Righteousness is not just about personal holiness but about embodying faith in action through love and service.

Piety acts as a cohesive element in spiritual formation, linking other virtues. With daily devotional practices that form the backbone of **Piety**, individual faith can stay cohesive, and communities can maintain the unity that binds them together in purpose.

Piety provides the discipline and routine necessary for believers to engage with their faith consistently. Through prayer, reflection, and acts of service, believers develop a sustained relationship with God, creating a foundation that supports other spiritual practices. Therefore, a disciplined approach to devotion is not an optional or secondary aspect of faith; it sustains spiritual growth in both personal and communal contexts.

In Latine traditions, **Piety** often manifests in Marian devotions, prayers, and veneration of saints, providing regular touchpoints with God. These forms, such as the recitation of the rosary or participation in *Las Posadas*, emphasize the relational aspect of faith, where devotion is expressed individually and communally. As Conde-Frazier points out, these rituals serve as a means of cultural and spiritual identity, grounding believers into a dynamic and traditional faith.[12] In this way, **Piety** is the foundation upon which other core virtues can flourish, providing the discipline needed to sustain a vibrant spiritual life.[13]

Latine religious traditions embody lived **Piety**, seamlessly integrating devotion into daily life through practices like the *Rosario* (Rosary) and *Las Posadas*. The *Rosario*, a central Catholic devotion in Hispanic/Latine communities, offers a structured way to meditate on Christ's life and the Virgin Mary through repetition and reflection. *Las Posadas*, a nine-day Mexican celebration reenacting Mary and Joseph's search for shelter, blends prayer, processions, and festive gatherings, symbolizing faith's communal and celebratory nature. These traditions illustrate how spiritual devotion is deeply woven into cultural identity, reinforcing faith through ritual, reflection, and shared experience. For instance, the veneration of the Virgin Mary provides an avenue for continuous spiritual reflection and ties with God through a profoundly emotional and ritualistic practice. Marian devotions, such as *Las Posadas* or the *Rosario*, are communal acts that strengthen faith while uniting families and communities. These disciplines infuse routine life with moments of prayer, humility, and devotion, illustrating how **Piety** can transform the mundane into a sacred rhythm of life. The constant repetition of these rituals in Latine cultures adds flavor to what might otherwise become monotonous or stale. Through such traditions, believers maintain a living, dynamic attachment with God, keeping their spirituality fresh and relevant daily. These devotional habits are more than just traditions; they are spiritual lifelines that keep faith active and alive, ensuring that **Piety** anchors believers through the highs and lows of life.

Incorporating Indigenous rituals into daily reflections or rituals, such as the veneration of saints alongside native symbols, reflects a form of syncretism that is deeply embedded in the religious life of many Latin American Christians. This blending of traditions highlights how **Piety**, far from being purely imposed, becomes an active form of cultural and spiritual preservation, allowing believers to sustain their correlation to their ancestral roots even within Christian frameworks.

In the kataphatic/affective quadrant, **Piety** is situated in a space that emphasizes emotional engagement and devotion. This quadrant reflects the importance of mediation and personal relationship with God, not through intellectual exercises but through feeling and engagement with the heart. **Piety** is not just about a structured routine but about engaging one's emotions in relationships with others and God. Through these daily acts of devotion, believers experience God's presence on a personal level, creating an ongoing, lived relationship that nourishes the soul.

The Argument for Piety as Centrality

Through the lens of Latine traditions, **Piety** demonstrates how essential daily devotional traditions are to maintaining an active, vibrant faith. Without **Piety**, spiritual practices become disconnected from the daily realities of life, and the other blocks lose their grounding. Through daily acts of devotion, believers continually realign their hearts and minds with God's will, allowing for sustained spiritual growth and resilience. Integrating collective rites and personal reflection, **Piety** enhances humility, compassion, and sustained engagement with the sacred. Thus, **Piety** remains central to spiritual growth, ensuring a vibrant view of God and community across generations and cultural contexts. Community prayers, saint veneration, and Marian devotions illustrate the essential role of **Piety** in nurturing a rooted spirituality with communal faith. These practices unite believers through shared worship, cultural identity, and reverent devotion, emphasizing prayerful living as a cornerstone of spiritual life.

The Role of Personal Reflection

Solitude, the practice of retreat and introspection, allows believers to connect in a deeply personal and vulnerable way. John of the Cross, one of the great mystics of the church, used periods of **Solitude** to reflect on his relationship with God, producing works like *Dark Night of the Soul*, which continue to inspire believers seeking wisdom through introspection.[14] In this sense, Solitude is about creating space for personal encounters with God, where one's identity and purpose can be explored in the light of grace.

René Terranova, a Pentecostal theologian, speaks to the importance of **Solitude** as a sacred space for spiritual renewal and preparation for spiritual warfare.[15] For Terranova, periods of **Solitude** and reflection allow believers to encounter God more intimately, confront inner struggles, and emerge with greater clarity and strength for the mission ahead. This view aligns **Solitude** with personal introspection and as a necessary step in spiritual empowerment and preparation for service.

Elizondo adds to this by highlighting how **Solitude** and reflection are integral to the process of *mestizaje*, where cultural and spiritual identities are formed at the intersection of different experiences.[16] **Solitude** becomes a time for spiritual reflection and personal and cultural identity exploration. Holmes speaks to this by framing **Solitude** in the apophatic (mystical) dimension of spirituality, where the absence of clarity allows for a more profound encounter with God.

In today's fast-paced world, filled with endless distractions and demands, the importance of **Solitude** as a vital component for spiritual clarity cannot be overstated. Far from being merely quiet, Solitude involves purposefully withdrawing from the community—stepping away from everyday relationships and responsibilities—to reconnect with God and recalibrate one's internal compass. In these moments apart, the clutter of daily life fades, enabling individuals to listen more attentively to the whispers guiding their paths.

Integrating **Solitude** into one's spiritual practice is indispensable for maintaining spiritual health and cultivating one's relationship with God. Without these moments of personal reflection, spiritual practices risk becoming shallow and disconnected from the believer's inner life.

In Latine spirituality, **Solitude** is often intertwined with nature. Pilgrimages, retreats, and moments of silence in sacred spaces provide opportunities for personal reflection and engagement with God and Creation. This practice of **Solitude** sustains emotional and spiritual clarity, much like in Nancy Pineda-Madrid's reflections on Latina spirituality, where moments of stillness provide space for healing and renewal.[17] **Solitude** is not a withdrawal from the world but a retreat that enables believers to return to their communities with renewed strength and purpose.[18] These traditions offer unique pathways for experiencing **Solitude**. Deep spiritual traditions, such as the Desert Mothers' and Fathers' disciplines and nature retreats, provide an enriching perspective on how personal reflection can cultivate one's participation in God. Many Latin American religious traditions intertwine this sense of reflection with a profound connectedness to the land. Pilgrimages to sacred spaces, time for personal reflection in nature, and solitary reflection amid the beauty of Creation bring an additional depth to contemplative practices. These traditions teach that **Solitude** is not isolation but a means of reconnecting with God and the natural world, grounding believers in their spiritual and physical environments.

Solitude in Latin America often involves deep reflection on cultural and spiritual identity shaped by centuries of colonial exploitation. As individuals retreat into **Solitude**, they seek a personal union and engage in a broader dialogue with their historical and cultural heritage, confronting the tensions between Indigenous roots and colonial legacies.

In the apophatic/affective quadrant, **Solitude** emphasizes emotional vulnerability and the opportunity to connect with the transcendent. **Solitude** is not simply about withdrawing from the world but about feeling deeply and being open to a presence without showing vulnerability to others. It is a time for believers to bear their hearts to God, trusting that they will find healing, guidance, and renewal in these quiet moments.

The Argument for Solitude as Sacred Space

Solitude is not merely an absence of noise or community but a sacred space where the soul encounters God in its most vulnerable and transformative state. Far from isolation, **solitude** is a deliberate withdrawal that allows individuals to recalibrate their spiritual compass, confront inner struggles, and find renewed strength for engagement with the world. In many traditions, **solitude** is intertwined with nature, pilgrimage, and contemplation, offering a space for personal transformation and a reorientation toward justice and community. In these moments apart, the distractions of daily life fade, making way for deeper introspection, healing, and openness to guidance. Reflection in **solitude** also shapes identity, where the tensions between personal experience, cultural heritage, and faith are explored. The stillness of these sacred moments brings emotional clarity and spiritual resilience, providing the necessary grounding to return to daily life with renewed purpose and conviction. Reclaiming **solitude** as a holy space is essential for cultivating a personal and communally transformative faith in an age of constant noise and distraction.

Justice and Ethical Living

Rectitude is the moral backbone of faith, emphasizing justice and integrity as central elements of Christian spirituality. Óscar Romero, who sacrificed his life for the sake of the poor in El Salvador, is a prime example of this virtue in action.[19] His commitment to justice was unwavering, even in political persecution. Gebara extends this understanding of **Rectitude** to include gender justice, calling the church to confront patriarchy and advocate for the dignity of all people, especially women.[20] Gutiérrez defines morality as an essential part of liberation theology, where faith must be lived out to pursue justice for the people facing oppression.[21] His option for the poor reflects a deep commitment to aligning Christian ethics with social justice, where ethical living leads to active engagement in the world.[22] Miguel A. De La Torre's concept of "ethics from below" challenges dominant power structures and encourages believers to act ethically in solidarity with marginalized communities.[23]

Rectitude is foundational for Christianity to remain relevant and connected to the world's pressing issues. With a focus on ethical living, Christian practice can avoid becoming insular and disconnected from the real needs of personal and societal contexts.[24]

Samuel Solivan emphasizes that **Rectitude**, particularly in Hispanic Pentecostal theology, is deeply tied to the pursuit of justice and liberation for individuals from marginalized backgrounds.[25] He argues that the empowerment of the Holy Spirit compels believers to act against injustice, making the pursuit of social and moral **Rectitude** inseparable from Christian spirituality. This understanding positions **Rectitude** as a personal virtue and a call to transform society through active engagement in justice, particularly in the face of systemic oppression. **Rectitude** is not merely an optional spiritual practice—it is essential for transforming the individual and the community, grounding Christian life in ethical living, justice, and compassion. In today's world, where inequity and injustice prevail, **Rectitude** serves as a moral compass, guiding believers toward actions that reflect the heart of the gospel.

In Latine traditions, **Rectitude** is often embodied in activism and advocacy. Whether through marches, protests, or community organizing, pursuing justice is a fundamental expression of faith. Conde-Frazier also emphasizes the role of education in promoting justice, arguing that **Rectitude** requires believers to advocate for change and educate themselves and others about systemic oppression.[26] This form of righteousness goes beyond personal morality and becomes a social responsibility, where faith and justice are inextricably linked. **Rectitude** finds a powerful expression in liberation theology, which originated in Latin America and offers a justice-oriented Christianity rooted in advocacy for the poor and people facing oppression. This theology embodies the principle that true Christian faith must involve action for individuals from marginalized backgrounds. In this context, spiritual integrity is not confined to personal morality but extends to social justice, addressing systemic inequality and advancing a more just world. The Latine commitment to community advocacy, especially the fight for the dignity of the poor, is an essential ingredient in the modern spiritual diet. This tradition offers a tangible example of how **Rectitude** translates into real-world activism, inspiring Christians to live out their faith through justice-oriented action.

The Argument for Rectitude as a Path to Transcendence

Rectitude occupies the apophatic/cognitive quadrant, which focuses on knowing without possessing and emphasizes the capacity to act justly based on wisdom. This quadrant challenges believers to pursue justice not for personal gain but as a reflection of their commitment to God's transcendent nature. When aligned with principles, the intellectual pursuit of justice transcends individual motives, leading to actions that resonate with a higher moral calling. Therefore, **Rectitude** is understanding justice and practicing right relationships aligned with justice, ensuring that ethical living remains central to spiritual practice.

Theological Foundations for a Dynamic Spirituality

A robust spiritual life extends beyond personal sanctity, actively shaping the individual and the world. Within Latine theology, the dynamic interplay of virtues of **MPSR** highlights spirituality that is at once contemplative and engaged in concrete solidarity. Gutiérrez and Ellacuría remind us that faith detached from suffering becomes stagnant, whereas integrating introspection with action offers a living testimony to God's redemptive work. Consequently, spiritual growth must be incarnational, contextual, and socially transformative, uniting the mystical with the practical.

Gutiérrez reorients theology toward solidarity and praxis in his articulation of the preferential option for the poor, asserting that genuine faith must be lived out in response to social injustice. Spiritual disciplines, much like the **MPSR** framework, must nourish the inner life of the believer and their engagement with the world's suffering. **Piety** without **Rectitude**, for instance, risks becoming a detached spirituality that neglects justice, while **Majesty** without **Solitude** may appear as rigid dogmatism without self-reflection. Gutiérrez calls for a faith that integrates these elements—a contemplative spirituality actively engaged in justice-seeking praxis. Ellacuría expands this vision by reframing spirituality as a force for historical transformation. His call to "take charge of reality" underscores that saints—those seeking a flourishing spiritual life—cannot retreat from the world's injustices but must instead use their spiritual formation to effect real change. This aligns with the transformative nature of **MPSR**, where each virtue is not merely a private discipline but a communal, prophetic force that influences both

Box 3.2 The Transformative Power of Faith in Action

A robust spiritual life is not merely about personal sanctity but a catalyst for transformation that shapes both the individual and society. The interplay of **MPSR** within the framework of Latine theology highlights that true faith must be both mystical and practical, grounding believers in spiritual depth while compelling them toward justice and solidarity.

Liberation theology teaches that Christians cannot remain passive in the face of injustice—faith must be lived through active engagement, where personal integrity and societal justice become guiding forces. **Rectitude**, particularly within Latine traditions, is not an abstract virtue but a justice-driven practice—a call to ethical living that directly confronts inequality and oppression. Spirituality that separates itself from the struggles of the world risks stagnation, while one that integrates reflection with action becomes a living testimony of God's redemptive work.

the individual and society. **Majesty** fuels the courage to challenge unjust structures, **Piety** sustains an interplay with God and others, **Solitude** cultivates the clarity needed for discernment, and **Rectitude** ensures that action is morally grounded.

Listening to the voices of Gutiérrez and Ellacuría, it becomes evident that a flourishing spiritual life must engage both personal transformation and collective mission. Spirituality must be dynamic, contextual, and responsive to the evolving needs of communities. Latine spiritual traditions, which emphasize communal celebration, devotion, reflection, and justice, offer a compelling model for integrating these principles into daily life. Such practices prevent spiritual stagnation and cultivate resilience, purpose, and a faith that actively participates in God's mission of justice and liberation. Therefore, sainthood is not an abstract ideal but a lived reality that calls believers to cultivate spiritual depth while embodying faith through compassionate service, moral courage, and communal transformation.

Chapter Four

Majesty

The Lord *answered Samuel, "Comply with the people's request—everything they ask of you—because they haven't rejected you. No, they've rejected me as king over them."*

—YHWH (1 Sam. 8:7 CEB)

In this chapter, the focus shifts to **Majesty**, the building block and the first essential element in cultivating a spiritual diet. **Majesty** is like salt in the context of sainthood, representing God's sovereignty and grandeur, which inspires awe and reverence in our lives. As we embark on this chapter, we explore how recognizing the good in others nourishes our souls, blending virtues like humility, wisdom, and compassion—deeply rooted in Latine traditions of reverence for saints and communal acts of faith. This recognition of good is not passive; it actively shapes our interactions and enhances our relationship with God. It uplifts us and fills us with hope, knowing that goodness exists and can be a powerful force for spiritual growth with humility.

Majesty = Queen / King = Salt

As salt enhances a meal, **Majesty** cultivates our reverence. A leader's crown is not forged from power but from humility.

- Learns life from the front
- Guides with authority and purpose
- Uses sovereignty and governance
- Is an example of sacred authority

As we proceed, we will witness the transformative power of **Majesty** when blended with the other theological foundations of sainthood—**Piety**, **Solitude**, and **Rectitude**. This blend provides a holistic framework for spiritual growth, particularly relevant to the culturally rich Latine experience. Just as salt enhances flavor, **Majesty** guides reverence for God's kinship, grounding us in purpose, authority, and humility. It inspires spiritual transformation, catalyzing profound change and filling us with motivation.

A Lesson in Grace and Responsibility

Once there was a noble ruler known for his fairness and wisdom. A troubled farmer approached him as he sat in his grand hall one morning. With worry etched on his face, the farmer explained that his neighbor had borrowed money some time ago but refused to repay the debt despite repeated reminders. Desperate for a solution, the farmer turned to Count Lucanor, seeking guidance. Lucanor's wisdom and compassion shone in this moment, providing a guiding light for those in need. He listened carefully, then turned to his trusted adviser, Patronio, who always had a story to share when wisdom was needed. Patronio began, "My lord, once in a distant land, a mighty king ruled his kingdom with great justice. One day, a poor citizen came to the king with a similar problem. A wealthy merchant owed him a significant sum but refused to pay. At his wit's end, the citizen asked the king for help."

Patronio's voice was calm as he continued, "The king, rather than immediately punishing the merchant, devised a different plan." He invited both the citizen and the merchant to a grand banquet. At the feast, the merchant was given the seat of honor and served the finest dishes in the kingdom. The food was plentiful, the wine flowed, and the merchant, feeling meaningful and joyful, thanked the king profusely for his generosity. After the feast, the king approached him as the merchant was about to leave. Calmly, he said, "As you have enjoyed the riches of my table, so must you fulfill the debts you owe in life. Gratitude must be followed by responsibility, just as you have received, so you must give back what is due." Humbled by the king's wisdom and the weight of his conscience, the merchant immediately paid the citizen what he owed.

Lucanor leaned back in his chair, absorbing the lesson in Patronio's tale. With a thoughtful nod, he turned to the farmer. "Approach your neighbor not with anger, but with grace. Remind him gently of the value of honor and responsibility. Speak to him not as an enemy but as a fellow man who must uphold his word." Following the count's advice, the farmer returned to his village and spoke to his neighbor kindly, reminding him of their bond as men of integrity. Moved by the farmer's approach, the neighbor repaid the debt and peacefully resolved the conflict. The count had once again shown that true wisdom lies not in force but in guiding others to see their duties with humility and grace.

As Lucanor reflected on Patronio's tale, he recognized a worthy lesson in leadership. The king had not resolved the issue through force but through gentle authority, reminding the merchant of his duty with grace and subtle wisdom. Lucanor understood this was the essence of **Majesty**—not in dominance but in the ability to guide others with humility and dignity.

True leaders, like the king, use their influence to uplift others. Figures such as Chávez, who fought for justice for farmworkers, and Archbishop Óscar Romero, who spoke out against oppression, exemplify this form of **Majesty**. They led compassionately, advocating for individuals from marginalized backgrounds and inspiring others to act with integrity, empowering us and giving us hope for a better future. Much like the servant-king, the count demonstrates that a leader's crown is forged not from power but from humility—a quality that guides others through grace and authority. In this understanding, Lucanor saw that his role as a leader was not merely to resolve conflicts but to inspire others to fulfill their responsibilities with honor. Faithful **Majesty** embodies learning from life directly, guiding with authority and purpose, and exemplifying valid sacred authority. Blending sovereignty with wisdom, **Majesty** seeks to elevate those needing guidance, motivating us to act with honor and integrity.

A Theological and Latine Perspective

In the introduction, I noted that while Rolheiser advocates mellowness, Gutiérrez argues that **Majesty** also requires righteous anger and boldness against injustice. Jesus's example with the children is that he "was angry with his disciples" (Mark 10:14 NLT). **Majesty** in Christian theology involves awe and empowerment for transformative action. It reflects grandeur and authority, manifesting through leadership characterized by humility, justice, and spiritual wisdom—revealing God's sovereign power through service, compassion, and sacrificial love. This boldness highlights the intersection of authority and human dignity in a spiritual diet.

Non-Latine theologians Karl Barth, Hans Urs von Balthasar, and Jürgen Moltmann each illustrate a different facet of **Majesty**. Barth highlights God's sovereignty through Christ, whose reign redeems and transforms.[1] Balthasar approaches Majesty through aesthetics, perceiving splendor in the beauty of revelation.[2] Moltmann's *The Crucified God* presents Majesty in suffering and vulnerability, revealing power through redemptive self-giving.[3]

In contrast, majesty includes the moral responsibility to uplift marginalized communities in a Latine context. For instance, Chávez, through his leadership of the United Farm Workers, demonstrated spiritual grandeur by championing justice and dignity for grape laborers.[4] Óscar Romero embodied majesty in his prophetic opposition to oppression, a stance that ultimately led to his assassination.[5] Garcilaso de la Vega extended majesty into the cultural sphere, bridging Indigenous and Spanish heritages in his writings and challenging imperial authority.[6]

Table 4.1 Theologians' Perspectives on Majesty

Theologian	Cluster	Perspective on Majesty
Barth	Non-Latine	Sovereignty through Christ's rule and transformation
Balthasar	Non-Latine	Beauty and glory of revelation
Moltmann	Non-Latine	Power in suffering and vulnerability
Chávez	Latine	Advocacy for justice and dignity
Romero	Latine	Prophetic justice and sacrifice
De la Vega	Latine	Cultural majesty and shared heritage

Latine theologians define **Majesty** as an attribute and a leadership model that embodies humility and justice. This perspective integrates authority with a commitment to serve the people facing oppression, positioning **Majesty** as a spiritual and social transformation force.

Biblical Models of Majesty

Following this understanding of **Majesty**, the biblical stories of Joseph in Egypt (Gen. 39:1–20) and Daniel in Babylon (Dan. 1:1–8:26) serve as powerful biblical examples of sacred authority grounded in wisdom, humility, and authority. These men, though living in times of hardship—Joseph during slavery and Daniel during exile—demonstrated **Majesty** by using their positions not for personal gain but to elevate others and fulfill God's greater purpose. Like salt enhancing a dish, their decisions revealed how **Majesty** amplifies the sacred. Their reverence for God's sovereignty grounded their leadership, guiding their actions with humility and moral courage.

Joseph, sold into slavery and later rising to power in Egypt, exemplified **Majesty** through his ability to interpret dreams and manage resources with foresight and wisdom (Gen. 41:39–41). Rather than seeking revenge or power, Joseph used his authority to save Egypt and his siblings who betrayed him (Gen. 45:4–7). His leadership, like that of the king in Lucanor's story, was marked by compassion and a deep sense of responsibility to serve others. Similarly, though taken into exile in Babylon, Daniel gained the trust of kings through his unwavering faith and prophetic insight (Dan. 6:1–3). Daniel's **Majesty** lay in his refusal to compromise his beliefs while still serving the foreign rulers with integrity (Dan. 1:8–9). Like Joseph, he used his position to guide and protect his people, showing that authentic leadership often arises under challenging circumstances.

Joseph and Daniel embody the biblical concept of **Majesty**—leading with wisdom, faith, and a commitment to others' well-being, even amid adversity. Like Chávez and Archbishop Romero, their stories illustrate that salty **Majesty** lies not in dominance but in guiding others with humility, compassion, and responsibility.

The Bible also offers profound insights into **Majesty** as an ingredient for spiritual sustenance. In 1 Samuel 8:7, God's response to Israel's desire for a king reminds us that faithful **Majesty** belongs to God alone: "They haven't rejected you. No, they've rejected me as king over them" (CEB). This passage highlights the importance of recognizing God's sovereignty in all aspects of our lives, as human attempts to claim **Majesty** often fall short of the model. Spiritual nourishment comes from acknowledging that God's **Majesty** is the ultimate authority that guides us in our personal and communal lives.

Majesty in the Life of Jesus

Jesus used his authority as salt that flavored his teachings and actions, showing that authentic sacred authority is rooted in humble service. His life and ministry are perfect examples of living out authority with humility, sovereignty, and governance. God "sent [him] to preach good news to the poor" (Luke 4:18 CEB). Through his actions, teachings, and how his followers understood him, Jesus embodied **Majesty**—not as a ruler seeking power but as a servant leader showing us how to care deeply for others.

Unlike the Sadducees, whose authority was rooted in hierarchy rather than humility, Jesus showed **Majesty** through a different kind of sacred authority—embodying authority and mission to serve others, particularly individuals from marginalized backgrounds. Jesus understood **Majesty** as something rooted not in dominance but in service to others. In Mark 10:45, Jesus said, "For even the Son of Man did not come to be served, but to serve, and to give His life as a ransom for many." This profound statement sets the tone for his entire ministry: Jesus, as the King of kings, did not rule with an iron fist but with a servant's heart. He used his authority to uplift the downtrodden, heal the sick, and proclaim freedom to oppressed people (Luke 4:18–19). His understanding of **Majesty** was countercultural, as it involved self-sacrifice and a deep commitment to the well-being of others. This servant-leadership culminated in washing his disciples' feet in John 13:12–15. By performing this humble task, Jesus showed that faithful **Majesty** is not found in a position of power but in acts of love and humility. He told his disciples, "I have set you an example that you should do as I have done for you" (John 13:15), emphasizing that the highest form of leadership is not about dominance but about transformative service that uplifts and empowers.

Jesus taught his disciples about love and demonstrated it through tangible actions. One of the most significant examples is the feeding of the five thousand (Matt. 14:13–21). In this miracle, Jesus takes the humble offering of five loaves and two fish and multiplies them to feed a vast crowd. Here, Jesus shows how **Majesty** manifests in meeting the physical and spiritual needs of others with proper administration and action. His ability to take something small and use it to nourish many reflects the power to transform lives with love and generosity. This miracle perfectly illustrates how **Majesty** works through the principle of abundance. Jesus uses the elements of compassion, grace, and provision to nourish the souls of those he encounters from what he has available from his sovereignties. His ministry was an ongoing demonstration of feeding the body and spirit, ensuring that those who followed him received the sustenance they needed to grow in faith and love.

The New Testament contains examples of how Jesus's followers recognized his **Majesty**. In Matthew 16:16, Peter declares, "You are the Messiah, the Son of the living God," acknowledging Jesus's unique role as the one who would lead them to redemption. Similarly, in John 6:68, Peter again proclaims, "Lord, to whom shall we go? You have the words of eternal life." The disciples saw Jesus not just as a teacher or prophet but as the embodiment of authority, a trustworthy source of spiritual nourishment.

Even after his resurrection, Jesus continued demonstrating his **Majesty** by empowering his followers to carry forward his mission. In Matthew 28:18–20, Jesus proclaims, "All authority in heaven and on earth has been given to me. Therefore, go and make disciples of all nations." His disciples understood that this **Majesty** was not about self-glorification or a nationalistic gospel but about extending the love and grace of God to all people. Like a master chef sharing his recipe, Jesus gave his disciples the tools to spread love, forgiveness, and compassion worldwide with definitive action. Jesus's life and ministry are the ultimate recipe for loving others. He took the theological foundations and showed his followers how to use them to create a life of service, compassion, and integrity.

Jesus has given us the start to a perfect recipe: Love deeply, serve humbly, and lead compassionately (Mic. 6:8). This is the prophetic essence of spiritual nourishment, and through his life, we are invited to craft a robust spiritual diet that reflects the same love and grace he so generously shared with the world.

Teresa of Ávila and Majesty

Similarly, Teresa of Ávila's reforms exemplify the governance of sacred authority, showing how embracing God's **Majesty** brings purpose to one's leadership. Through her reforms, she became a leader who, like a sovereign, led with moral courage and humility. Teresa of Ávila, the renowned Spanish mystic, theologian, and reformer, provides an exemplary model of how **Majesty** can serve as a vital ingredient in the spiritual diet for nourishment. Through her profound mystical experiences, the reform of the Carmelite order,[7] and her development of *El Castillo Interior* (*The Interior Castle*), Teresa articulated a deep understanding of **Majesty** as a source of spiritual sustenance, helping believers grow in humility, wisdom, and grace while walking with God. Her life and works highlight how spiritual nourishment involves recognizing God's **Majesty** within oneself and extending that realization into loving service and reform at a time when a woman's voice was not heard.

Born in 1515, Teresa of Ávila lived during an era of significant religious and cultural upheaval, marked by the Protestant Reformation and growing calls for reform within the Catholic Church. Although the Carmelite order originated on Mount Carmel centuries earlier—ultimately forced to relocate to Europe in the thirteenth century due to conflicts associated with the Crusades—the order was well established in Teresa's day. Yet it faced new challenges, including complacency and lax discipline in some monasteries.

Therefore, Teresa's decision to reform the Carmelite order and establish the Discalced Carmelites was bold. She encountered intense opposition from church authorities and local communities who resisted change. Undeterred, Teresa leaned on a profound sense of **Majesty** grounded not in external power but in humility and obedience to God's sovereign will. While still requiring official church approval, she famously stated, "Humility must always be doing its work like a bee making its honey in the hive: without humility, all will be lost," underscoring her belief that true greatness lies in self-effacement and reliance—not in asserting dominance.[8]

This humility, deeply rooted in her understanding of **Majesty**, allowed her to, through these challenges, establish it as a resilient and adaptive order within the broader landscape of Catholic spirituality. She consistently integrated her mystical experiences into her leadership, offering a vision of spiritual life that was as practical as it was profound. Teresa's ability to articulate her vision for reform, integrate it into her daily spiritual practices, and collaborate with others in the church demonstrates the power of **Majesty** as a force for personal and communal transformation.

The Interior Castle has been regarded as one of the most significant works in Christian mysticism. E. Allison Peers describes it as "a masterpiece of spiritual psychology," emphasizing its depth in guiding the soul toward union with God through contemplation and prayer.[9] As Teresa's masterpiece, *El Castillo Interior* provides a detailed framework for understanding how the soul progresses toward union with God. A castle with seven distinct mansions symbolizes the pilgrimage. Each mansion represents a different stage of spiritual development, beginning with the most external focus on worldly concerns and culminating in the most profound, intimate union with others and God. On the other hand, Caroline Walker Bynum explores how Teresa's work reflects the sociopolitical challenges of her time, particularly in its depiction of spiritual progression as resistance to external distractions and worldly attachments.[10] Both scholars highlight *The Interior Castle*'s continued relevance in theological studies, offering insights into the nature of spiritual growth and the soul's intimate relationship.

Teresa discusses the soul's awakening to God's presence in the first three mansions and the early struggles with temptation and distractions. The soul, still entangled in worldly desires, begins to recognize God's **Majesty** but lacks the full integration of authority into everyday life. Teresa notes the importance of humility during this phase, emphasizing that without it, progress is impossible. She famously said, "It is love alone that gives worth to all things," reminding her readers that **Majesty** is expressed through love and humility, foundational to spiritual growth.[11] Gutiérrez applies these principles by encouraging us to draw from our own spiritual resources while working to liberate the people facing oppression.

As the soul moves deeper into the castle, through the fourth, fifth, and sixth mansions, it begins to experience God's **Majesty** fully. These stages involve increasing degrees of contemplation, spiritual ecstasy, and surrendering the self to God's will. Teresa describes the experience of God's grandeur as overwhelming and transformative, a clear reflection of **Majesty** in its purest form. She described the soul as being in a realm of immense grandeur, comparable to a place where the sun's brilliance is so intense that it overwhelms one's vision. This encounter with **Majesty** nourishes the soul, allowing it to shed its attachment to lesser things and focus entirely on God.

In the seventh and final mansion, the soul reaches the complete union with God, entirely participating in the life. Teresa describes this stage as one in which the soul, now fully integrated with **Majesty**, becomes a vessel for God's will on earth. The person who reaches this stage embodies authority, leading others by example and spreading God's love and grace through their actions. Teresa described this transformative union as a state of profound peace and joy in which the soul remains entirely still and rooted in its bond with God. Grande exemplifies this revolutionary inspiration, as his ministry's commitment to justice and liberation ultimately led to his assassination.

Among Latino theologians, Elizondo and Orlando Espín have engaged with Teresa of Ávila's mysticism and theology, particularly in how her spirituality resonates within the Latin American context.[12] Elizondo draws parallels between Teresa's experience of deep spiritual moments with God and the communal experiences of marginalized peoples in Latin America, where suffering and spirituality are deeply intertwined. Espín, in his exploration of popular religiosity, highlights Teresa's profound influence on the devotional practices of Latin American Catholics, emphasizing how her teachings on humility, contemplation, and **Majesty** provide a spiritual framework for resistance and hope among people facing oppressive communities. These theologians acknowledge Teresa's continued impact on Latine spirituality, underscoring her relevance to contemporary faith, identity, and social justice issues.

Teresa's leadership in reforming the Carmelite order demonstrates how **Majesty** can be articulated, integrated, and collaborated upon in pursuing spiritual and social renewal.[13] Despite opposition from religious leaders and societal norms, Teresa of Ávila remained steadfast in her belief that reform was essential for the church's spiritual renewal. Her efforts to revitalize the Carmelite order, emphasizing prayer and discipline, played a crucial role in its transformation. For an in-depth exploration of her reforms, *The Carmelite Tradition* by Steven Payne provides historical and spiritual context, while *The Life of St. Teresa of Avila by Herself* offers firsthand insight into her motivations and experiences. Teresa's unwavering commitment continues to inspire spiritual renewal and devotion. Her ability to articulate this vision in her writings and actions reflects a clear understanding of **Majesty**—an authority rooted not in human ambition but in God's will.

Teresa integrated her mystical insights into the daily customs of the Discalced Carmelites, emphasizing deep prayer, contemplative silence, and communal support. Her reforms in a tumultuous time focused on stripping away the excesses and distractions of monastic life, returning the order to a focus on simplicity and devotion. She believed this simplicity allowed for a more evident encounter with God's **Majesty**, nourishing the soul and strengthening the community.[14]

Collaboration was also a key component of Teresa's success. She worked closely with figures like Juan de la Cruz, who shared her vision for reform and supported her efforts. Together, they created a spiritual movement that transformed the Carmelite order and impacted the broader church.[15] Her life demonstrates how **Majesty**, combined with humility and love, can overcome immense obstacles and lead to profound spiritual and social change.

Teresa's life, writings, and reforms offer timeless lessons on how **Majesty** can nourish the soul. Her famous quote "Let nothing disturb you, let nothing frighten you, all things are passing away: God never changes. Patience obtains all things. Whoever has God lacks nothing; God alone suffices" reflects her deep trust in the sacred and her understanding of God's **Majesty** as a source of strength and nourishment.[16] This legacy invites saints to incorporate salty **Majesty** into their spiritual lives as a foundation for humility, wisdom, and transformative leadership.

In the Latine theological tradition, Teresa of Ávila's insights reflect a vision of Majesty as authority and the responsibility to uplift others. Her reforms of the Carmelite order embodied this harmony, emphasizing prayer and spiritual renewal. Teresa's legacy inspires faith by integrating contemplation with the call to uplift and transform communities. Just as she revitalized her community through reform, **Majesty** still guides spiritual leaders in weaving together faith, culture, and social justice, promoting growth that uplifts individuals and society.

Building a Diet for Sustenance

Majesty acts as a key ingredient in our pilgrimage toward spiritual wholeness, showing up in personal moments of devotion and broader expressions of faith that lead us closer to fullness in Christ. Much like salt—an unassuming element that has shaped societies and economies—Majesty subtly enriches our relationship with God and the world, adding depth and purpose. By uniting these theological insights, historical reflections, and contemporary disciplines, we construct a stable spiritual "diet" that fortifies us from within, ensuring our faith remains nourished and transformative over time.

Garcilaso de la Vega, known as "El Inca," provides a powerful example of how **Majesty** can be understood culturally and spiritually.[17] In his work *The Florida of the Inca*, Garcilaso bridges the Indigenous and Spanish worlds, using his dual heritage (Inca and Spanish) to craft a narrative that honors both. This cultural integration reflects diversity and the blending of spiritual and cultural identities. Just as Garcilaso sought to elevate the lives of Inca heritage while embracing his Spanish identity, we too must integrate different aspects of our spiritual lives into a cohesive whole. This kingly integration of cultural and spiritual reverence invites us to draw from diverse spiritual traditions to enrich our spiritual diet. Supporting the wisdom of our ancestors and contemporary practices, we honor the fullness of God's **Majesty.** God was with them as much as God is with us today. The **Majesty** of God calls us to embrace a symmetrical spiritual pilgrimage that honors the richness of our heritage and the beauty of diversity.

Antonio Vieira, a Jesuit priest known for his powerful sermons, emphasized the governance of eloquent leadership and moral authority.[18] His sermons (sometimes preached to fish), rich with rhetorical brilliance, called for protecting Indigenous people and reflected a deep commitment to justice and human dignity. Vieira's understanding of **Majesty** was rooted in his conviction that authentic leadership must serve others, particularly those facing oppression. He was a prominent political adviser to King John IV of Portugal, who valued Vieira's intelligence and diplomatic skills. Vieira's bold ideas and unorthodox views often put him at odds with the Portuguese court, especially after the Restoration War, when Portugal regained independence from Spain in 1640. Drawing from Vieira's example, we can see how the **Majesty** of God nourishes us through our call to serve and uplift others. As part of our spiritual diet, **Majesty** is not simply about recognizing God's grandeur but also about embodying that grandeur in our actions. Vieira's life was filled with personal sacrifices. His work often involved traveling between Europe and Brazil, enduring difficult conditions, and facing poor health. Vieira's sermons remind us that spiritual sustenance comes from contemplation and active engagement in the world—especially in defending individuals from marginalized backgrounds. Despite these struggles, Vieira left an enduring legacy. His sermons and letters are regarded as masterpieces of the Portuguese Baroque period, and his commitment to social justice, intellectual freedom, and religious tolerance remains celebrated today. In this way, our spiritual diet must fuel inward reflection and outward action, ensuring that we live out God's **Majesty** daily.

In his seminal work *For the Life of the World*, Alexander Schmemann presents the sacred rituals as central to the Christian experience of God's **Majesty.**[19] For him, the sacred rituals are not merely rituals but encounters that transform the mundane into the holy. The Eucharist, for example, is a moment in which believers partake in the **Majesty** of Christ's sacrifice and resurrection, experiencing the fullness of grace through the physical elements of bread and wine. His emphasis on sacramental life offers a powerful model for understanding how **Majesty** sustains us. The sacred rituals nourish us spiritually, connecting us to the reality that underpins all Creation. They invite us to see the world as charged with God's presence, where every moment has the potential to reveal "the awesome splendor of God" (Job 37:22 CEB). In our spiritual diet, the sacred rituals serve as essential nourishment—reminders that we are sustained not just by prayer and reflection but by the tangible experiences of God's **Majesty** in the world around us.

In *The Universal Christ*, Richard Rohr challenges us to see Christ's **Majesty** not as confined to specific religious experiences but as a universal reality that permeates all Creation.[20] Rohr emphasizes that Christ is present in every aspect of life, from the most minor acts of love to the grandest cosmic events. This expansive view of Christ's **Majesty** calls us to recognize the divine in all things, breaking down the barriers between the sacred and the secular.

Rohr's vision of an expansive **Majesty** invites us to craft a spiritual life that embraces both the extraordinary and the ordinary. Just as physical nourishment comes from diverse sources, spiritual nourishment involves recognizing God's presence in every moment. Whether in prayer, work, or rest, the **Majesty** of Christ calls us to live with an awareness of the sustaining presence. This perspective shifts us from compartmentalized methods to an integrated life infused with **Majesty**.

At the heart of a truly nourishing spiritual life is the grandeur of God's **Majesty**, a cornerstone that enriches every aspect of our being. Drawing from the wisdom of Garcilaso de la Vega, San Antonio de Vieira, Alexander Schmemann, and Richard Rohr, we see that a balanced spirit draws on many traditions, serves others, honors sacred rites, and encounters Christ everywhere—sustained by the constant flow of God's **Majesty**. This spiritual sustenance does not hinge on a single practice but permeates every moment of life, empowering us to live fully in the presence of God. As Teresa of Ávila taught, "It is love alone that gives worth to all things." We find the sustenance for our spiritual pilgrimage through the **Majesty** of God's love. Embracing **Majesty** as a critical element in our spiritual lives invites us to experience the fullness of God's grace, love, and authority in all we do.

Majesty as a Core Element of Spiritual Transformation

The four theological foundations illustrate how these essential components create an aligned spiritual life. Each foundation represents a unique aspect of spiritual practice, and together, they form a holistic framework for transformation. As a foundational element, **Majesty** embodies authority and grandeur, guiding our pilgrimage. Like a master chef balancing flavors, **Majesty** blends these components to nourish the soul and support spiritual growth.

Majesty is not merely an isolated spiritual concept but the bedrock upon which the other essential theological foundations are constructed. This building block inspires and shapes our understanding of **Piety**. When we recognize God's grandeur and authority, our worship, prayer, and devotion are transformed into genuine expressions of reverence and humility. **Piety** becomes more than ritual; it is a heartfelt response to the overwhelming awe we experience when encountering God's **Majesty**. This recognition elevates our spiritual approaches, ensuring they acknowledge God's sovereignty.

In Latine spiritual traditions, this correlation between **Majesty** and **Piety** is reflected in communal acts of devotion, such as reverence for saints or Marian apparitions. These practices are grounded in the understanding of authority, where acts of **Piety** are imbued with a sense of **Majesty**. Thus,

Table 4.2 Comparative Perspectives on Majesty in Christian Theology

Theological Tradition	Key Concept of Majesty	Example Figures	Impact on Spirituality
Catholicism	Anointed sovereignty as a guiding force in church doctrine and liturgy	Teresa of Ávila, Thomas Aquinas	Majesty is expressed through structured worship and ecclesiastical authority
Protestantism	Personal relationship with God's Majesty through Scripture	Martin Luther, John Calvin	Emphasis on God's authority over individual faith
Liberation theology	God's Majesty as liberation for the oppressed	Gutiérrez, Romero	Calls for justice and social transformation as acts of reverence

Majesty shapes not only individual purity but also the collective spiritual identity of communities, linking devotion with the grandeur of God. Also, **Majesty** serves as the foundation for true **Solitude**. Recognizing God's authority and power enables us to enter vulnerable spaces of introspection with confidence and trust. **Solitude** allows for deeper communion with God, but our awareness of **Majesty** provides the inner strength necessary to embrace these applications. Knowing that we are held by a presence more significant than ourselves, we can approach **Solitude** with humility and courage. Teresa of Ávila's mystical experiences exemplify this bond. Her deep understanding of God's **Majesty** allowed her to embrace **Solitude** as a transformative practice, trusting that God's grandeur would guide her through moments of vulnerability and challenge. Her life teaches us that **Majesty** is not distant or overpowering; instead, it is a source of comfort and strength that nurtures our spiritual growth.

Moral **Rectitude** rests on **Majesty**, the authority shaping our moral order. Recognizing God's sovereignty empowers just, humble, and ethical living, as seen in Romero's unwavering commitment to truth under persecution. **Majesty** is the cornerstone of faith, guiding **Piety**, **Solitude**, and **Rectitude. Majesty** elevates all virtues, as seen in Daniel, Joseph, and Jesus's transformative leadership. Without it, faith loses focus; with it, we mirror God's sovereignty and serve others. Garcilaso, Antonio, and Teresa show how cultural and spiritual **Majesty** enriches faith, nourishing self and community: Interplaying with **Majesty** as our bedrock forges a resilient spirit—like a crown refined by fire—rooted in humility, compassion, and justice.

Chapter Five

Piety

A Priest—whoever he may be—is always another Christ.

—St. Josemaría Escrivá

In this chapter, we begin by introducing the next essential spiritual building block: **Piety**. This chapter invites us to explore how recognizing and amplifying the goodness in others can serve as a powerful form of spiritual nourishment. **Piety** resembles the enriching essence of fat in a dish, warming our devotion as daily rain nourishes the fields. Faith often arises from small, compassionate acts that cultivate ties, depend on people and intercession, and embody Levitical service. **Piety** is not grand but integrated into daily life, emphasizing humility and service to amplify goodness.

Piety = Priest = <u>Fat</u>

As fat enriches a dish, **Piety** warms our devotion. Devotion waters the soul like daily rains nourish the fields.

- Cultivates interplays
- Depends on people
- Enhances intersession
- Lives Levitical service

This chapter introduces recognizing the good in others as the second building block of a spiritual "diet," nourishing the soul by enhancing our connection to others and God. In the Latine experience, where spirituality blends ancient wisdom with contemporary practices, it manifests in actions that uplift individuals and society. Like fat enriching a dish, **Piety** sustains and amplifies our spiritual lives through compassion, devotion, and imitation of Christ. Guided by the Holy Spirit, integrating **MPSR**, we create a holistic approach to sainthood rooted in cultural and communal modes.

A Tale of Piety and Devotion

In a humble village in Latin America, a modest juggler dreamed of performing on a grand stage, perhaps in a magnificent cathedral like the Basilica of Our Lady of Guadalupe. His heart brimmed with hopes of fame, fortune, and the admiration of countless spectators. Day after day, he rehearsed tirelessly, envisioning himself dazzling the crowds with his skills. When the moment finally arrived, he traveled to the bustling city, only to be met with indifference. His carefully crafted tricks, meant to amaze and inspire, were met with scornful laughter. The applause he had longed for dissolved into sneers, and the grandeur of his dreams shattered, leaving him dejected.

Seeking solace, the juggler wandered into the peaceful refuge of the basilica. Standing in awe before the image of the Virgin of Guadalupe, he felt a quiet peace there. The crowd's cruelty faded in the presence of the Holy Mother's gaze, and his disappointment gave way to a different longing—a desire to offer her the best of what he had. In the quiet of the basilica, far from the clamor of the outside world, he began to juggle—not for the crowd but as an offering of devotion to the Virgin herself. Each ball toss became a prayer, each movement an act of reverence.

As days turned into weeks and weeks into months, his juggling ceased to be a performance for others. It transformed into a sacred ritual, a quiet offering with pure love and faith. In his quiet devotion, something miraculous happened. The Virgin revealed herself to him, her face filled with grace and compassion. She acknowledged the sincerity of his heart, blessing his humble offering. In her eyes, his act of devotion, born from a place of love and faith rather than a desire for praise, was far more valuable than the cheers of any crowd. From that moment on, the juggler's life changed. No longer did he seek the fleeting applause of an audience. His performances were now only for the Virgin, each movement guided by her invisible hand. What once had been a pursuit of recognition became a sacred dance of **Piety**, a joyful expression of his love for her. He found fulfillment not in worldly accolades but in the quiet presence of the Holy Mother, who accepted his simple gift with boundless grace.

Piety is the art of being, not merely doing. The *cuento* of the juggler passed down through generations reminds us of the true nature of devotion. In a world that often celebrates showiness and grandeur, humble acts of love, done with sincerity and faith, hold the most profound value. The story teaches us that **Piety** is found not in the spectacle but in our quiet, pure offerings to God and those we love. Even the simplest gestures, when given with a sincere heart, are blessings in the eyes of the anointed. The juggler's story reveals how **Piety** provides warmth and sustenance to a faith-based life. His simple act of juggling became, through devotion, a rich offering, transforming his ambitions into spiritual sustenance.

Fat is a powerful flavor carrier, intensifying and distributing flavors throughout dishes. Each type of fat, such as butter, olive oil, or sesame oil, contributes unique flavors to a dish. We see a profound link to the core virtue of **Piety**—a devotion rooted in humility and sincerity, much like the sacred role of a priest in the way these actions contribute to our spirituality. Josemaría Escrivá's words, "A Priest—whoever he may be—is always another Christ," remind us that true priesthood is not confined to formal titles or grand gestures but to the inner transformation of the heart. Like a priest offering his daily acts of worship, the juggler's humble performance before the Virgin becomes his offering, his act of devotion mirroring the role of Christ through his pure intentions. As a priest stands before God on behalf of the people, the juggler, in his quiet and unexpected acts of faith, stands before the Virgin with nothing but his simple gift of love. In this way, he becomes "another Christ," embodying a life of service, **Piety**, and grace. His offering, small in the eyes of the world, becomes monumental in the eyes of God—teaching us that **Piety** is about the purity of our devotion, not the grandeur of our actions.

From Personal Discipline to Communal Compassion

In examining the essence of saintly **Piety**, we discover that true devotion is not confined to solitary acts of discipline but flourishes in a dynamic conversation between personal rigor and a heartfelt commitment to communal well-being.

Saints who practiced **Piety** believed in strict personal discipline and intense prayer to connect with God when exploring the spiritual world. They sometimes used ascetic practices like fasting and keeping night vigils, believing these acts would help purify the soul from sin. At the same time, they paid close attention to the sincerity of every prayer and good deed, teaching that the right inner intention could bring a person closer to the divine. Repentance was also a big part of their lives, and they often looked for ways to atone for their sins, including accepting suffering as a path toward spiritual growth. However, they weren't just focused on themselves; they also cared deeply about helping their communities. They taught that everyone should share responsibility for each other's well-being—if someone sinned or was in trouble, the entire group felt it. In everyday life, charity, kindness, and honesty mattered as much as praying and fasting.

They studied sacred texts to guide them, seeking a balance between strictly following every commandment and showing compassion to those around them. Through this combination of personal devotion, communal concern, and the careful study of the word of God, they hoped to honor God in all areas of life. This **Piety** sees spirituality as a personal, ongoing conversation with God rather than just a set of rules to follow. God is not distant or impersonal but is a loving presence who reaches out to each of us. When we encourage ourselves to listen to God's call in our daily lives, we learn from our experiences and allow that relationship to change the way we see ourselves and the world around us.

This message is that genuine engagement grows through honest reflection, a readiness to forgive, and a commitment to live with compassion. Our walk of faith is about more than rituals—it is about transforming our hearts and actions. In God's love, we can find the strength to face life's challenges and the motivation to care for others. This work for the saint teaches that every hardship is a chance to learn and grow and that we can contribute to a more just and caring world by nurturing our inner life. **Piety** reminds us that spirituality is a vibrant, lifelong adventure where hope and love guide every step.

A Theological and Latine Perspective

Just as an abuela's prayers nourish her family with consistency and love, daily acts of **Piety** ground believers, infusing spiritual life with warmth and sustaining integration through devotion, prayer, and Marian traditions. While Rolheiser highlights personal morality, from a liberation theology perspective, **Piety** should manifest in communal acts of solidarity and service, together with justice alongside devotion, as Ellacuría, Gutiérrez, Romero, and others have claimed. In theological terms, **Piety** refers to a deep passion, spiritual fervor, and religious dedication expressed through personal commitment to God. It is not limited to outward rituals but rooted in an intimate relationship with the eternal, leading to an integrated life of faith and action. Across Christian traditions, **Piety** has been interpreted in various ways, reflecting both mystical and practical dimensions of devotion.

The Latine tradition often expresses **Piety** through personal devotion, community action, and cultural identity. Figures such as Toribio Motolinía and Bartolomé de las Casas saw **Piety** as inseparable from pursuing justice for oppressed people.[1] De las Casas expressed this by defending Indigenous peoples, arguing that true **Piety** requires a commitment to human dignity and social justice. This reflects a preferential option for the poor, where devotion to God manifests in solidarity with marginalized communities.

Piety is more than personal devotion; it is the bridge that connects inner faith with outward action. A faith that is lived out fully does not remain within the confines of private spirituality but flows into communal life, inspiring acts of service, justice, and compassion. True **Piety** is a dynamic force, sustaining a profoundly personal and communal spirituality. Through this integration, faith becomes transformative—guiding individuals and communities toward a life marked by love and justice.

Latine **Piety** is deeply communal and often expressed through public acts of worship, such as processions, fiestas, and pilgrimages. It is also rich in symbolism and tied closely to cultural elements like the veneration of the Virgin. For Latine believers, **Piety** is an inward expression of faith and

Table 5.1 Piety as a Bridge between Devotion and Action

Aspect of Piety	Expression in Personal Life	Expression in Community	Theological Implications
Prayer	Daily spiritual discipline	Corporate prayer, liturgical practices	Deepens relationship with God
Service	Acts of kindness and charity	Church-based outreach and missions	Faith as action
Sacraments	Participation in the Eucharist, baptism	Collective rituals supporting unity	Marks spiritual identity and transformation
Justice	Advocacy for the marginalized	Faith-based activism	Aligns **Piety** with social ethics

a lived practice of solidarity and service, as demonstrated by Robert Chao Romero and Marcos Canales in their work on the faith witness of figures like de las Casas. In this tradition,[2] **Piety** is a driving force for social change, where devotion to God cannot be separated from the defense of people with lived experiences of marginalization. While **Piety** in the broader Christian tradition reflects a blend of personal spirituality and public action, it is uniquely communal and tied to cultural identity and justice in Latine communities. **Piety** in this tradition calls for personal faithfulness and collective efforts to transform society through love, service, and advocacy for the poor, changing their textures.

Biblical Models of Piety

In the biblical narratives of Joseph in Egypt (Gen. 39:1–20) and Daniel in Babylon (Dan. 1:1–8:26), we find compelling examples of **Piety**—acts of deep devotion and trust in God, even when faced with overwhelming hardship. First, Joseph in Egypt (Gen. 37–50) illustrates **Piety** through his unwavering faith despite betrayal, slavery, and imprisonment. Sold by his siblings and taken to Egypt as a slave, Joseph never abandoned his trust in God. Even when falsely accused by Potiphar's wife and thrown into prison, he remained steadfast, refusing to succumb to bitterness or despair. His ability to interpret dreams (Gen. 40:8, 41:16) was a gift he consistently acknowledged as coming from God, saying to Pharaoh, "It is not in me; God will give Pharaoh a favorable answer" (Gen. 41:16 ESV). Joseph's actions were infused through every trial with **Piety**—quiet devotion, trusting that God was working through him, even when others did not see or acknowledge it.

Joseph's most significant example of **Piety**, however, came from his forgiveness of his siblings. After being elevated to a position of power in Egypt, he could have sought revenge, but instead, he reassured them, "You intended to harm me, but God intended it for good to accomplish what is now being done, the saving of many lives" (Gen. 50:20). Joseph's humility, forgiveness, and trust in God's more excellent plan, despite years of suffering, are the hallmarks of his **Piety**.

Similarly, Daniel in Babylon (Dan. 1–6) exemplifies **Piety** during exile. Daniel was taken from his homeland and placed into the king's service, yet he resolved to remain faithful to God in every aspect of his life. When asked to eat the royal food and wine, which would have violated his dietary laws, Daniel respectfully refused, asking for vegetables and water instead (Dan. 1:8–16). Even in such small matters, his devotion exemplified his dedication to God. This act of **Piety** led to God's favor, as Daniel and his friends appeared healthier than those who had eaten the royal food (Dan. 1:15). Daniel's most famous **Piety** act occurred when a decree was passed prohibiting prayer to anyone except the king. Daniel prayed thrice daily with his windows open toward Jerusalem (Dan. 6:10), even though it placed him in mortal danger. His refusal to stop praying, even when faced with the lion's den, demonstrated his unshakable trust in God. His faith was rewarded when God sent an angel to shut the mouths of the lions (Dan. 6:22), leading King Darius to declare, "For he is the living God and he endures forever; his kingdom will not be destroyed, his dominion will never end" (Dan. 6:26).

Joseph and Daniel show us that **Piety** is about not grand displays of devotion but a consistent, quiet faithfulness that honors God in every circumstance. Like the juggler who offered his simple talent to the Virgin, Joseph and Daniel's small acts of devotion—interpreting dreams, following dietary laws, and maintaining prayer routines—became powerful witnesses to God's faithfulness. Their stories remind us that **Piety**, like fat, increases satiety by digesting slowly, enhancing the sensory experience, and creating a satisfying, complete meal. It is not about public acclaim but about remaining faithful to God, trusting that God sees and rewards even the humblest acts of faith.

Piety in the Life of Jesus

In the grand narrative of spiritual nourishment, Jesus's ministry on earth can be a perfect model of how **Piety** is a personal act of faith and a dynamic force that manifests in our love and care for others. Jesus didn't just teach **Piety**—he lived it, embodying perfect love in every interaction, healing, and teaching, showing us how to blend life's spiritual "ingredients" into a perfect dish of love.

Unlike the Pharisees' performative **Piety**, true devotion is nourished like fat in Levitical offerings, and it warms and grounds worship in daily acts of faith. In this sense, priests intercede for others through practices that cultivate a personal and communal resonance with God. Jesus's understanding of **Piety** is revealed in his consistent devotion to God, primarily through prayer and acts of compassion toward others. Throughout the Gospels, we see that Jesus prioritized his relationship with the Father through regular prayer, often retreating to solitary places to commune with God (Luke 5:16). This shows that **Piety**, for Jesus, was not about public displays of righteousness but about an intimate and continuous relationship with God.

One clear example of Jesus teaching **Piety** is found in the Sermon on the Mount, where he instructs his followers, "But when you pray, go into your room, close the door and pray to your Father, who is unseen. Then your Father, who sees what is done in secret, will reward you" (Matt. 6:6). Jesus taught that true **Piety** is private, sincere, and rooted in the heart rather than performed for public approval. He contrasted authentic **Piety** with the performative righteousness of the Pharisees, saying, "Do not be like the hypocrites, for they love to pray standing in the synagogues . . . to be seen by others" (Matt. 6:5). Through his actions, Jesus demonstrated that **Piety** is not an external show but an inner devotion that reflects outwardly in acts of love and kindness. The root of this **Piety** is the link with God, which fuels how we treat others, just as in the metaphor of this book, where spiritual practices are described as the essential theological foundations of a holistic "diet." Jesus shows that **Piety** is the foundation for a life that nourishes others with grace and love.

Jesus's ministry is filled with acts of **Piety** that seamlessly blend love for God and love for neighbor. Throughout the Gospels, he ministered to individuals from marginalized backgrounds, showing how true devotion to God manifests in serving those often overlooked. In the feeding of the five thousand (John 6:1–14), Jesus does not merely perform a miracle to demonstrate his power. He acts out of deep compassion, understanding the physical and spiritual hunger of the people. He embodies the very **Piety** he taught, offering bread for their bodies and the Bread of Life for their souls.

Another powerful example is the healing of the leper in Mark 1:40–45. Lepers were outcasts, cut off from society, and considered unclean. Yet Jesus, driven by **Piety** and compassion, reaches out to touch the man, saying, "I am willing. . . . Be clean!" (Mark 1:41). His **Piety** was not confined to the temple or the synagogue but was lived out in the streets, in personal interactions with individuals from marginalized backgrounds, showing that true devotion to God is inseparable from love for others. Just as a master chef blends ingredients to create a dish that nourishes body and soul, Jesus's ministry combined compassion and devotion to feed the deep needs of those around him.

Jesus's followers recognized his **Piety** through his teachings and way of life. The apostles and disciples often marveled at his prayer life to the Father. In Luke 11:1, a disciple asks, "Lord, teach us to pray," recognizing Jesus's profound relationship with God and wanting to share in that same devotion. Jesus then taught them the Lord's Prayer (Luke 11:2–4), offering a model of **Piety** that blends worship, repentance, and reliance on God.

In washing the disciples' feet (John 13:1–17), Jesus once again demonstrated the heart of **Piety**—humility in service. Though he was their master, he humbled himself, performing a task typically reserved for the lowest servant. He told them, "Now that I, your Lord and Teacher, have washed your feet, you also should wash one another's feet" (John 13:14). Jesus's followers saw firsthand how true **Piety** is expressed through selfless acts of love and service. His ultimate act of **Piety**, the sacrifice on the cross, culminated in his devotion to God and his love for humanity. Paul summarizes this beautifully: "He humbled himself by becoming obedient to death—even death on a cross!" (Phil. 2:8).

Reflecting on Jesus's life and ministry, it becomes clear that he exemplified the perfect blending of **Piety**, love, and service. His devotion to God was the foundation for everything he did, and his acts of love toward others were the natural outpouring of that relationship. Jesus used the spiritual "ingredients" of devotion, compassion, and humility to show us how to live a life that genuinely nourishes others. For those seeking to cultivate a spiritual life rich in **Piety**, Jesus provides the ultimate example. He teaches us that **Piety** is not merely about prayer and personal devotion but about how those practices lead to lives of radical love and service. As we blend the spiritual, theological foundations in our lives, Jesus's life becomes our model—a recipe for sainthood accessible to all who seek to love God and others with sincerity and humility.

In the context of this book's theme, Jesus invites us to craft a spiritual diet rooted in **Piety**—much like how fat binds ingredients and creates stability in cooking—nourishing our souls and those around us. Learning from Jesus, we are called to embody his example of love, devotion, and service in every aspect of our lives.

Bartolomé de las Casas and Piety

Bartolomé de las Casas exemplifies how **Piety**, rooted in deep devotion, nourishes the soul and society. His advocacy for Indigenous people in Latin America illustrates **Piety** as a "spiritual fat" that enriches and sustains justice and love. He exemplifies how **Piety**—rooted in spiritual fervor and ethical responsibility—can become a transformative force for justice and societal change. His life's mission to defend the Indigenous peoples of the Americas against the brutalities of La Conquista offers a powerful example of how **Piety**, as an essential spiritual "ingredient," nourishes both the soul and the broader community. De las Casas did not merely process personal devotion; his understanding of **Piety** was inseparable from his commitment to social justice, embodying a model of articulation, integration, and collaboration that changed the course of history.

A faith that does not confront injustice betrays itself. De las Casas's commitment to justice was not limited to theoretical discourse; he sought to integrate his faith with practical advocacy. His concept of "intercession for the Indians" became a cornerstone of his spiritual mission. He interceded on behalf of the Indigenous peoples before the Spanish monarchy, convincing King Charles V to enact "The New Laws of the Indies" in 1542, which sought to limit the exploitation of native peoples.[3] Though these laws were not fully enforced due to resistance from colonists, de las Casas's work represents a remarkable example of integrating faith with political and social advocacy. De las Casas's shift from complicity in oppression to defending

Indigenous rights shows that true **Piety** demands confronting injustice, not just private devotion.

In this work, Gutiérrez situates Bartolomé de las Casas as a key historical figure whose defense of Indigenous peoples prefigures central themes in liberation theology, particularly the commitment to confronting systemic injustice in the name of Christian faith.[4] De las Casas consistently argued that true Christian **Piety** required the defense of the people facing oppression. In his sermons and writings, he emphasized the preferential option for the poor—a concept that resonates deeply within Latine theology. His work prefigured liberation theology's insistence that faith without justice is empty. For de las Casas, **Piety** meant standing alongside the people facing oppression, and he saw his advocacy as a natural extension of his devotion to God. As he argued, "The conversion of souls is impossible without first restoring their humanity."[5] He also understood that he needed to collaborate with secular and religious authorities to bring about real change. He worked tirelessly within the Catholic Church, presenting his case before theologians and clergymen and often facing significant opposition. His most famous debate was with Sepúlveda, who argued that the Indigenous peoples were "natural slaves" according to Aristotle's philosophy. De las Casas countered with theological arguments based on the dignity of all humans as children of God, stating, "The Indians are our siblings, and Christ gave his life for them."[6]

Though de las Casas did not always succeed in implementing his reforms, his ability to collaborate with others, including sympathetic members of the clergy and monarchy, led to significant changes in the conversation around colonization. His work contributed to the eventual abandonment of the *encomienda* system[7] and paved the way for future Indigenous rights advocates. De las Casas's most well-known quotes, such as "All the world is human" and his critique of the Spanish colonizers as committing "unforgivable offenses against God and man," reflect his understanding of **Piety** as inseparable from the fight for human dignity.[8]

In the context of this book's metaphor of spiritual nourishment, de las Casas demonstrates how **Piety** can be a crucial ingredient in sustaining both the individual soul and the larger community. His life shows that **Piety**, when properly understood, is not passive devotion but active love, which seeks to restore dignity and justice. Just as a nourishing diet requires a blending of ingredients to sustain the body, spiritual **Piety** involves the integration of devotion, justice, and service to others. Articulating the plight of the Indigenous, integrating his faith with action, and collaborating with others to bring about change, de las Casas provides a model for holiness that nourishes the soul and the world. His life reminds us that **Piety**, when practiced holistically, can be a transformative force for good, providing the sustenance necessary to challenge injustice and uphold the dignity of all people.

The Core Ingredient for Sustaining Spirituality

Juan de la Cruz reflects the mystical tradition of **Piety**, where devotion is focused on an intimate, transformative relationship with God. Clare, a follower of Saint Francis of Assisi, lived a life of poverty and prayer, her **Piety** sustained through a deep sense of God's presence in her everyday life. Her **Piety** was characterized by simplicity and humility, nourishing her soul through a life of self-denial and service. In his work *The Dark Night of the Soul*, de la Cruz explores the more challenging aspects of **Piety**, where the soul undergoes spiritual desolation before reaching union with God.[9] This aspect of **Piety** teaches that spiritual nourishment is not always comforting; it often involves trials that purify the soul. Clare and John exemplify how **Piety** brings joy, service, and a willingness to endure suffering for spiritual growth. Their lives remind us that a spiritual diet includes sweetness and bitterness—consolation and purification.

Juan's mystical theology emphasizes that true **Piety** integrates contemplation, ethical engagement, and spiritual growth. **Piety** appears in many forms—from intellectual devotion and active service to pursuing justice and mystical union with God. Genuine faith cannot be divorced from ethical engagement, as caring for the marginalized and confronting oppressive systems are part of the believer's responsibility. At the same time, prayer and reflection empower outward works, creating a cycle where personal devotion and public witness mutually reinforce each other. Central to this method is recognizing that spiritual growth often involves consolation and hardship, leading to a more resounding communion with God.

In the pilgrimage of faith, let **Piety** be the sustaining fat that unites the devotion of the heart, the firm ground of **Majesty**, the profound silence of **Solitude**, and the guiding reality of **Rectitude**—turning private glorification into a living testament of justice and love. Figures like Bartolomé de las Casas—and communal traditions such as fiestas and Marian dedications—show how **Piety** outperforms private worship to bring meaningful change to individuals and societies. Working in concord with the other three blocks, **Piety** completes this balanced spiritual "diet," nourishing the soul and cultivating a love that radiates outward to transform communities.

Chapter Six

Solitude

But there is greater comfort in the substance of silence than in the answer to a question.

—Thomas Merton

This chapter invites us to explore **Solitude**, a crucial building block in cultivating a spiritual diet. **Solitude** is more than isolation; it is an intentional space that encourages introspection, clarity, and self-acceptance in the presence of God. Inspired by Juan de la Cruz, this chapter shows how stillness can nourish and transform, cultivating our spiritual pilgrimage. Recognizing goodness in others is fundamental to a spiritual diet. In Latine contexts, where community and family are central, affirming the good in those around us strengthens our bond with God.

Solitude = Mystic = Acid

As acid sharpens flavor, **Solitude** brings clarity. The whispers of truth become a roaring river in the silence of **Solitude**.

- Uses introspection
- Dedicates time to internal acceptance
- Discerns identity in the forge
- Accepts vulnerabilities

This recognition is not merely a practice but a source of profound spiritual nourishment that uplifts our souls. It embodies the communal aspect of spirituality, where personal growth intertwines with how we uplift others.

Blending this recognition with other theological foundations forms a holistic and nourishing spiritual life.

Solitude sharpens our focus, like acid sharpening a dish, revealing clarity and a grounded sense of identity. This **Solitude** is not emptiness but a space filled with introspection, acceptance, and discernment, where the sacred resonates. **Solitude** sharpens, **Solitude** clarifies, **Solitude** transforms. It uses introspection, dedicates time to internal acceptance, and discerns identity in the forge, ultimately embracing vulnerabilities.

Latine spirituality thrives on blending tradition and innovation and recognizing the goodness in others. This aligns with communal values of solidarity, compassion, and mutual respect, raising critical awareness (for liberation is conscientization). Acknowledging and celebrating the good in others, we nourish our spirits and contribute to the flourishing of those around us. Thus, our spiritual diet becomes a source of personal and collective growth.

The Silent Wisdom of the King's Tree

Once, in a time long forgotten, there was a monarch whose wisdom was renowned throughout the land. Under his reign, the kingdom thrived, and his people enjoyed prosperity and peace. Stories of the king's unmatched insight spread far and wide, attracting scholars from distant regions, all eager to learn the secret behind his wisdom.

One day, a group of scholars gathered before the king. With great reverence, they asked, "Your Majesty, please share with us the source of your profound wisdom." The king said nothing. Instead, he rose from his throne, gesturing for the scholars to follow. Silently, they walked through the grand halls of the palace, past rooms filled with the kingdom's riches, until they reached a hidden door that led to a lush garden. The air was cool and fragrant, and a magnificent tree stood at the garden's center. Its branches stretched wide; its leaves cast a gentle shade across the ground.

The king stopped at the tree's base; his gaze steady as he looked up at its towering form. The scholars, puzzled by his silence, exchanged glances, waiting for him to speak. Minutes passed, then hours, yet the king remained silent. The scholars, once impatient for an answer, began to quiet themselves. They looked at the tree—its deep roots anchored in the earth, its branches reaching for the sky—and slowly, they understood.

Wisdom, like the tree, grows in silence. It is not rushed or forced but cultivated with time, patience, and reflection. By bringing them to this tree, the king showed them that proper understanding comes not from words but from stillness and observation. The scholars left the garden with newfound insight. The king's silent lesson was clear: Wisdom is not something to be given but discovered, nurtured quietly like the grand tree in the heart of the garden.

The tale of *The Silent Wisdom of the King's Tree* mirrors the core theme that wisdom often blossoms in stillness. Just as the scholars learned from the silent presence of the king and the tree, **Solitude** invites us to embrace moments of quiet reflection, where proper understanding can take root. **Solitude**, much like the silent king's lesson, teaches us that profound growth often occurs not through words or actions but in the still, contemplative spaces where we connect deeply with ourselves and the anointed. Much like the flavor-sharpening acid, the silence surrounding the king's tree serves as a metaphor for **Solitude** that clarifies and refines. In this stillness, introspection and self-acceptance emerge, embodying the power of **Solitude** as the soul's essential space for growth.

As the scholars stood before the majestic tree, they gradually understood the king's silent lesson. The tree rooted profoundly and grew tall, symbolizing wisdom cultivated in stillness. The king's silence echoed the teachings of figures like Juan de la Cruz and Guamán Poma de Ayala, whose most fantastic insights emerged from **Solitude**. The scholars realized that true wisdom often arises not from words or actions but from moments of quiet reflection. Like the sacred space of the garden, **Solitude** enhances introspection and personal transformation. In the stillness, the scholars grasped that wisdom, much like the tree's growth, is nurtured in silence, allowing spiritual and intellectual depth to flourish.

A Theological and Latine Perspective

Latine theology, deeply rooted in daily spiritual practices, emphasizes that **Solitude** is not just withdrawal but preparation. In this quiet introspection, as acid sharpens a dish, **Solitude** clarifies purpose, calls forth vulnerability, and prepares the soul to act in solidarity with others. Rolheiser's emphasis on emotional peace can be critiqued through the lens of Althaus-Reid, who challenges the notion that tranquility is always appropriate, especially in the face of oppression. **Solitude** must also be a space for righteous anger and prophetic action. As understood by various theologians, **Solitude** is the sacred space necessary for deep personal reflection and spiritual growth. It is often described as intentional isolation where the soul can connect with God, away from distractions.

Table 6.1 The Role of Solitude in Different Spiritual Traditions

Tradition	Purpose of Solitude	Practices	Theological Impact
Desert Fathers	Seeking his presence	Retreating into the wilderness, fasting	Spiritual purification
Monasticism	Contemplation and discipline	Silence, prayer, writing	Deepens theological insight
Mysticism	Union with God	Meditation, isolation	Experiential knowledge of God
Latine Spirituality	Reflective solitude for social action	Spiritual retreats, discernment	Grounds faith in justice

For Latine people, **Solitude** carries distinct cultural and spiritual meanings, often tied to communal yet solitary faith practices. Abuelita theology reflects how Latine grandmothers nurture their faith in **Solitude**, passing on spiritual wisdom through quiet, personal practices that enrich individual and collective spirituality.[1] Abuelita theology is the care of everyday faith of grandmothers (*abuelitas*) who through simple acts of love, prayer, and resilience impart spiritual wisdom and trust in God's care to their families. This teaching resembles Paulo Freire's contemplative reflections on dignity and liberation during oppression.[2] Freire argued that education is a revolutionary and inherently political act in this learning and teaching because it empowers individuals to critically question and transform oppressive systems, fighting for liberation and social change.

In other words, **Solitude** is the contemplative space where introspection sharpens, personal identity is strengthened, and spiritual clarity emerges. It functions not as a retreat from the world but as a necessary preparation for engaging with it, much like the silent moments Jesus spent in prayer before his acts of ministry (Mark 1:35).

Biblical Models of Solitude

Following the king's silent lesson, we turn to the biblical figures of Joseph in Egypt and Daniel in Babylon, who exemplify **Solitude** as a source of wisdom and transformation. Both men, separated from their people and thrust into foreign lands, experienced a profound isolation—not just physical but cultural and spiritual.

Joseph, sold into slavery and exiled from his family, faced years of **Solitude** in Egypt. During this period of isolation, his character was refined, and he grew in wisdom. His quiet perseverance and trust in God eventually led him from a prison cell to a place of prominence in Pharaoh's court (Gen. 41:37–44). Like the king's silent garden, Joseph's **Solitude** became a space for personal transformation and cultivating his spiritual insight.

Similarly, Daniel, living in exile under Babylonian rule, experienced **Solitude** as a foreigner in a land that did not share his faith. Though surrounded by the pressures of an unfamiliar culture, Daniel's **Solitude** allowed him to maintain his devotion to God. Through prayer and contemplation, he gained wisdom that elevated him to a position of influence and enabled him to interpret dreams and visions (Dan. 6:10–28). Like Joseph's, his story demonstrates how **Solitude** can build up resilience and spiritual depth even in adversity.

Like the scholars before the king's tree, Joseph and Daniel discovered that true wisdom and strength emerged from embracing **Solitude**. In the stillness of their lives, they connected deeply with God, allowing wisdom to guide them through trials and into positions of influence. These biblical examples illustrate that **Solitude**—whether in slavery, exile, or adversity—sharpens focus, brings clarity, and transforms vulnerability into growth, resilience, and spiritual insight.

Solitude in the Life of Jesus

Jesus modeled a rhythm where moments of quiet reflection were essential in preparing him for ministry. **Solitude** in Jesus's life, much like acid enhancing a dish, sharpened his focus on his purpose, balancing compassion with clarity for action. His life and ministry offer the perfect example of how **Solitude** facilitates profound love and service to others when integrated into one's spiritual practice. Through moments of isolation, intentional reflection, and personal communion with God, Jesus demonstrated that **Solitude** is not a withdrawal from the world but a preparation for serving it with greater compassion and wisdom.

Throughout the Gospels, Jesus takes on **Solitude** to commune with God and gather strength before significant moments in his ministry. For instance, after his baptism, Jesus withdrew into the wilderness for forty days of fasting and prayer (Matt. 4:1–2). This period of **Solitude** prepared him to face temptation and emerge spiritually stronger, fully equipped to begin his public ministry. **Solitude**, for Jesus, was a space for spiritual nourishment and clarity—a foundational aspect of the spiritual diet that he would later share with his disciples.

Jesus also modeled **Solitude** as a regular practice, often retreating to quiet places to pray. Mark 1:35 reads, "Very early in the morning, while it was still dark, Jesus got up, left the house, and went off to a solitary place, where he prayed." This rhythm of retreat allowed him to maintain an integration with the Father, replenishing his spirit to continue the work of healing, teaching, and guiding his followers. His use of **Solitude** as a tool for spiritual renewal demonstrates how essential this building block is in cultivating a life of love and service.

Even in the face of overwhelming demands, Jesus made time for **Solitude**, showing that love for others flows from a heart centered on God. Before choosing the twelve apostles, he spent an entire night alone in prayer (Luke 6:12–13), a decision that shaped the future of his ministry. Through these solitary moments, Jesus prepared himself to love and lead others with wisdom and strength. His followers too recognized the power of Jesus's use of **Solitude**. In Luke 5:16, it is noted that "Jesus often withdrew to lonely places and prayed." The disciples saw firsthand how this practice sustained his ministry, empowering him to love others deeply and without exhaustion. For Jesus, **Solitude** was not a means of escape but an integral part of his spiritual diet, allowing him to pour out love in the most demanding circumstances.

Beyond embodying **Solitude**, Jesus revealed that genuine love for others blooms from the depths of an intimate relationship with God. When asked about the greatest commandment, Jesus responded, "Love the Lord your God with all your heart and with all your soul and with all your mind" (Matt. 22:37). This commandment flows naturally into the second, "Love your neighbor as yourself" (Matt. 22:39). These teachings encapsulate the spiritual nourishment of **Solitude**—drawing near to God so that we may be filled with God's love and able to share it abundantly with others. Jesus also exemplified how **Solitude** prepares us to minister effectively. Before feeding the five thousand, Jesus sought **Solitude**, retreating to a remote place (Matt. 14:13). However, even when the crowds followed him, his **Solitude** enabled him to respond with compassion, teaching and spiritually and physically feeding them. Here, Jesus shows that **Solitude** equips us to serve others with energy and love, especially when faced with the overwhelming needs of the world.

Jesus crafted a proportionate life, blending moments of **Solitude** with active ministry. He demonstrated that **Solitude**, far from being a withdrawal from the world, is a vital ingredient in a life that reflects God's love. Jesus teaches us to love others more fully through **Solitude**, as God's presence continually nourishes us. His life and teachings remind us that **Solitude** is not an end but a means of becoming more like him—able to love and serve others with grace and compassion.

In my overarching narrative of *Art of Sainthood*, Jesus exemplifies how the theological foundations of **MPSR** work together to nourish the soul and prepare us for a life of love. Like acid in cooking, **Solitude** is an essential ingredient in our spiritual lives, infusing depth and clarity that empower us to love our neighbors as ourselves. Throughout his life, Jesus calls us to embrace **Solitude** not as a retreat but as a vital agent of growth, love, and transformation.

Juan de la Cruz and Solitude

Juan de la Cruz (John of the Cross), one of Christianity's most profound mystics, teaches that solitude is indispensable to spiritual transformation—a theme he develops in his celebrated poems and commentaries, especially *The Ascent of Mount Carmel* and *The Dark Night*. These writings remain a cornerstone of Christian mysticism, systematically outlining the purification process necessary for union with God. In these writings, Juan de la Cruz describes the stages of the soul's spiritual walk through the dark night, a period of profound inner turmoil and spiritual desolation when the soul feels abandoned by God. At this time, Juan was imprisoned in a small, dark cell in the Carmelite monastery in Toledo, Spain, where he endured physical suffering, isolation, and deprivation. This night, however, is not a place of despair but one of deep spiritual refinement.

Juan's life exemplifies the transformative power of **Solitude**. He teaches that **Solitude** is not merely an absence of others but a sacred space where the soul most profoundly encounters God. Through his suffering and **Solitude**, Juan crafted poetic art that spoke to the soul's pilgrimage toward God, illustrating how **Solitude**, even in crisis, can be a space for profound creativity and spiritual insight. His ability to articulate these experiences in poetry reveals how **Solitude** seeks to integrate spiritual wisdom and collaboration with grace.

Juan's concept of the dark night is a metaphor for the soul's experience of suffering and silence in the spiritual pilgrimage. In *Ascent of Mount Carmel*, however, he situates the purging of desires at an earlier stage—before the crucible of the dark night. The soul must first shed its imperfections to be ready for illumination. Juan writes, "To reach satisfaction in all, desire its possession in nothing. To come to possess all, desire the possession of nothing."[3] This stripping away of desires and attachments remains essential, reaching its fullest expression in solitude, where the soul is free from external distractions.

Through his suffering and **Solitude**, Juan crafted art that spoke to the soul's pilgrimage toward God, illustrating how **Solitude**, even in crisis, can be a space for profound creativity and spiritual insight.[4] His ability to articulate these experiences in poetic form reveals how **Solitude** seeks to integrate spiritual wisdom and collaboration with grace.

For Juan, **Solitude** becomes a space for transformation, especially in times of profound hardship. His life and writings illustrate how **Solitude** is an essential ingredient in the spiritual diet, nourishing the soul by articulating, integrating, and collaborating with grace. His concept of the dark night reminds us that **Solitude**, while often painful, is necessary for spiritual transformation. Through **Solitude**, the soul is stripped of its attachments, cultivates its relationship with God, and emerges nourished and transformed, ready to embody the love and grace it has encountered.

Juan's understanding of **Solitude** as a space for nourishment resonates with the spiritual diet. **Solitude**, like an essential ingredient, supports a deep reflection, vulnerability, and internal acceptance necessary for spiritual growth. By integrating **Solitude** into the spiritual pilgrimage, Juan shows how one can move through the dark night and emerge transformed, filled with the light of God's presence.[5]

Solitude as a Place to Sustain Spirituality

Solitude acts as mystic acid, sharpening spiritual clarity and providing the stillness necessary for introspection, emotional vulnerability, and discernment. This road map to sustained spirituality aligns with Latine practices, as **Solitude** offers a time to recalibrate and gain focus, preparing individuals to engage deeply in both personal and communal life. To continue, we return to Juan, whose dark night serves as a profound road map for understanding the role of **Solitude** in spiritual sustenance. His depiction of the night offers a step-by-step guide for navigating the periods of desolation and internal struggle that every soul encounters on its pilgrimage to the divine union. The text explains how the purification process of **Solitude** strips away the soul's reliance on superficial comforts and brings it closer to God. The **Solitude** described by Juan is not a barren wasteland but a crucible where spiritual growth and transformation occur. This makes dark night a unique and invaluable resource for those seeking to cultivate an engaging spiritual diet, as it highlights the necessity of enduring suffering and embracing **Solitude** as an essential ingredient in the path to holiness.

Unlike *The Living Flame of Love*,[6] which focuses on the soul's final union with God and the ecstasies of love, dark night addresses the raw, complex process of purification and transformation.[7] This focus on the arduous nature of spiritual growth makes the dark night particularly helpful for those grappling with **Solitude** as a pathway to holiness. Juan's writing makes the reader understand **Solitude** as a necessary stage of spiritual refinement—an ingredient that, although challenging to swallow, is indispensable in creating a robust spiritual diet. His approach to **Solitude** resonates with modern readers, particularly in a world where constant distractions draw us away from meaningful spiritual reflection.

This understanding of **Solitude** echoes the contemplative practices of Merton, whose works explore **Solitude** as the foundation for spiritual clarity and social consciousness.[8] He viewed **Solitude** as a means for personal growth and developing a sense of responsibility with others. In **Solitude**, he argues, we strip away the noise of the world and come to a clearer understanding of our role in the broader community. His well-developed sense of social consciousness and his insights into **Solitude** speak to the importance of balancing contemplation with action. This is particularly relevant for those cultivating a spiritual diet, as it underscores the need to ground ourselves in **Solitude** while remaining engaged with the world around us.

Within the Restoration Movement, Randy Harris[9] and Jackie Halstead[10] introduced contemplative practices into a tradition that historically emphasized activism and community. Both scholars highlight the importance of **Solitude** for spiritual depth and clarity. Harris has drawn on the insights of mystics like Juan to encourage Restorationist Christians to embrace **Solitude** as part of their spiritual diet, seeing it not as a retreat from the world but as preparation for more meaningful engagement with it.

In the Baroque period, figures such as Baltasar Gracián offer a practical approach to navigating life's challenges with introspection and action.[11] Gracián's work, often seen in political and social commentary contexts, offers a practical approach to navigating life's challenges. It also addresses the importance of cultivating wisdom in **Solitude**. Scholars such as Jeremy Robbins have placed Gracián within the broader context of Spanish Baroque literature, noting how his reflections on prudence and inner strength resonate with the themes of **Solitude** and contemplation found in the works of mystics like Juan.[12]

Additionally, historical figures like Francisco de Vitoria, Bartolomé de las Casas, and Luis de Molina approached **Solitude** as a spiritual practice and a social and theological reflection space.[13] De las Casas, for example, used **Solitude** as a time for deep reflection on the injustices faced by Indigenous peoples in the New World as he traveled from continent to continent. His **Solitude** was not merely a withdrawal from society but a period of intense moral and theological development that ultimately fueled his advocacy for Indigenous rights.

Similarly, mystics such as Teresa of Ávila, María de Ágreda, and Sor Juana Inés de la Cruz offer unique perspectives on **Solitude** and holiness.[14] Teresa presents **Solitude** as the soul's pilgrimage inward, moving through layers of distraction and attachment until it reaches the "interior castle" where God dwells. This vision of **Solitude** as a path to holiness, where the soul is purified and strengthened in its relationship with God, has been foundational for understanding the role of contemplation in spiritual life. Teresa's example shows how **Solitude** becomes a source of sustenance, nourishing the soul as it moves through spiritual trials and closer to union with God. This approach—as seen in the writings of Juan, Merton, and others—shows that **Solitude** is a critical ingredient in the spiritual diet. It provides the necessary space for purification, reflection, and transformation, allowing individuals to grow closer to God and engage more deeply with the world. Whether approached through mysticism, contemplative prayer, or social consciousness, **Solitude** remains vital for sustaining a healthy and vibrant spiritual life.

Solitude as an Integral Building Block for Spiritual Transformation

As Figure 3.1 and this chapter illustrate, the essential theological foundations of **MPSR** form a dynamic framework for spiritual nourishment. Each quadrant represents a crucial aspect of spiritual life, and when integrated, they provide a comprehensive approach to personal and communal transformation. These blocks must work harmoniously, like the nutrients in a well-proportioned diet, to sustain a vibrant and healthy spirituality.

Majesty reflects the governance of the self, recognizing the grandeur of God and aligning our lives with God's will. **Piety** involves devotion and service that bring humility and cultivate our lives to God and others. **Solitude**, a space for vulnerability and deep reflection, allows us to retreat from the world's distractions and encounter the stillness. **Rectitude** provides the cognitive and moral foundation to guide our actions, ensuring that our spiritual practices are aligned with ethical living and integrity.

These theological foundations are not static; they flow into one another, creating a cycle of growth and transformation. **Solitude** nurtures the emotional and spiritual core, allowing **Piety** to flourish. **Majesty** provides the structure and order necessary to sustain **Piety**, and **Rectitude** ensures that both are anchored in wisdom and truth.

Solitude brings cohesion to other theological foundations of **Piety**, **Majesty**, and **Rectitude** in a holistic spiritual diet by ensuring that acts of devotion and service are carried out with intention and clarity. Latine spiritual traditions emphasize the rhythm of retreat and reengagement, where periods of **Solitude** are followed by active participation in community life. Grasping **Solitude**, individuals cultivate a sustainable spiritual practice that nourishes personal growth and the capacity to serve others.

As acid sharpens flavor, **Solitude** brings clarity. In its silence, whispers of truth become a roaring river, cutting through life's distractions and preparing us for deeper engagement with the world. **Solitude** is vital for personal renewal and collective spiritual growth. It uses introspection, dedicates time to internal acceptance, discerns identity in the forge, and embraces vulnerabilities. Like Jesus, who blended love, devotion, and service, we are called to craft a spiritual diet that sustains and transforms. Drawing from the rich traditions of Latine spirituality, we cultivate a life of deep faith, resilience, and communal flourishing.

Solitude as Sacred Space for Spiritual Clarity and Transformation

Far more than a withdrawal from the world, **Solitude** is a sacred space where spiritual clarity, transformation, and intimacy unfold. The **MPSR** framework serves as a crucible for deep reflection, enabling believers to refine their faith, confront inner struggles, and emerge with renewed purpose. Rather than isolation, **Solitude** represents intentional retreat and active engagement with God, the self, and one's spiritual calling.

Theologically, **Solitude** aligns with the mystical tradition, where silence and contemplation pave the way to unique encounters. Throughout history, spiritual figures have recognized that the soul can discern God's voice only in stillness. This introspection renews believers so they can reenter the world with clarity, conviction, and resilience. Without **Solitude**, faith risks becoming shallow and reactive, lost amid distractions. Yet when faithfully embraced, it anchors believers in discernment and heightened awareness of God's presence.

Practically, **Solitude** counters the constant noise of modern life, providing essential space for rest and reflection. In Latine traditions, this often occurs in pilgrimages, retreats in nature, or silent prayer woven into daily life. Such practices do not detach believers from the community; instead, they equip them to serve with wisdom and compassion. A spirituality lacking Solitude may lead to burnout and a loss of purpose, while too much **Solitude** risks detachment and escapism. Striking an interplay allows **Solitude** to become a wellspring of grounded faith—free from performative busyness and sustained by purpose and discernment.

According to Merton in *Thoughts in Solitude*, Solitude is more than being alone. It is a time set apart for deep inner listening.[15] When we choose solitude, we see ourselves honestly—our strengths, weaknesses, fears, and hopes. While facing these truths about us, we can learn to be humble, to let go of selfishness, and to discover a more authentic connection with God. Solitude also gives us a clearer sense of how we belong to one another and how we can serve those around us with genuine compassion. When we focus our hearts on what matters in these quiet moments of prayer and reflection, we practice stillness and simplicity so that God's presence can fill the space we create. Solitude becomes a tasteless drink of water that takes away unnecessary distractions and illusions. We find peace and a plunging trust in God's will in that refreshing drink of water. Far from making us distant or cold, solitude fills us with the courage and generosity we need to love and care for others. In other words, it transforms us and sends us back into the world as kinder, more honest, hydrated people.

Solitude cultivates relationships: It nurtures intimacy with God and self-understanding and empowers reengagement with others. This sacred pause strengthens convictions, restores the weary spirit, and clarifies the path forward. As we turn to **Rectitude**, we will see how Solitude undergirds ethical clarity, moral courage, and the pursuit of justice, ensuring spiritual formation translates into concrete action.

Chapter Seven

Rectitude

The Lord *is a warrior;*
the Lord *is his name.*

—Moses (Exod. 15:3 CEB)

As we approach the final building block of a spiritually nourishing life, we focus on **Rectitude**. While **Majesty** represents authority, **Piety** adds warmth, and **Solitude** is reflection, **Rectitude** strengthens the soul, binding all aspects of our spiritual pilgrimage. It embodies the moral fortitude that guides us on the path of justice, even when the road is steep. Rooted in strength and discipline, **Rectitude** calls us to live with integrity, equips us to take action, and challenges us to face life's obstacles head-on, grounding us like the roots of a sturdy tree in times of adversity.

Rectitude = Warrior = Heat

As heat binds all, Rectitude strengthens the soul. Justice is the path where integrity guides every step, even when the road is steep.

- Uses strength and discipline
- Lives out of integrity and capability
- Equips to get things done
- Challenges life
- Rooted in just relationships

In this chapter, we explore how **Rectitude** completes the spiritual diet by supporting a sense of righteousness that transcends individual morality and expands into communal justice. Drawing on Latine traditions of solidarity and resistance, we will see how embodying **Rectitude** nourishes not just the individual but the broader community. Ignacio de Loyola, a model of this virtue, exemplified the discipline of a champion of integrity, using strength to uphold righteousness in the service of others. His life reminds us that living with **Rectitude** means standing firm in our beliefs and navigating challenges with unwavering moral clarity.

Just as heat binds ingredients in cooking, **Rectitude** strengthens the soul, guiding every step with integrity on justice's path, even on the steepest roads. **Rectitude**, when blended with **Majesty**, **Piety**, and **Solitude**, creates a nourishing spiritual practice that reflects God's justice in the world. By recognizing the good in others and remaining steadfast in righteousness, we nourish our souls and uplift those around us, sustaining a community built on justice and integrity.

The Tale of the Ungrateful Snake

In a tranquil village nestled amid rolling fields, there lived a kindhearted farmer named Miguel, known throughout the region for his generosity and selflessness. One day, while working near the edge of his property, Miguel stumbled upon a wounded snake struggling in the grass. Without hesitation, he carefully scooped up the creature and carried it back to his humble home. Naming her Seraphina, Miguel tended to her wounds, offering her refuge and care. Seraphina became a constant presence in Miguel's life as time passed, bringing him an unexpected sense of companionship and joy. The villagers marveled at the sight of the farmer and the once-vicious serpent living in harmony. Despite this, a seed of doubt grew within Miguel's heart. He wondered if saving a snake, known for its unpredictable nature, had been wise.

One bright afternoon, Miguel's worst fears were realized. As he reached out to feed Seraphina, she turned on him, biting the hand that had saved her. The pain of betrayal stung deeper than the bite itself, and Miguel, wounded physically and emotionally, began questioning the price of his kindness. Gathering the village children around him, Miguel recounted his story, using it as a lesson about trust and caution. "Even the most harmless-seeming creatures," he warned, "can betray you when you least expect it." The tale of *La Víbora Ingrata*—the ungrateful snake—soon became a part of the village's folklore, passed down from generation to generation.

Some saw it as a warning against naive trust, while others reflected on the complexities of relationships, where betrayal can often come from those closest to us. Through the years, the fable has stood as a reminder that appearances can deceive and that even acts of kindness must be used with careful discernment. In countless villages across Latin America, the story of Miguel and Seraphina continues to be told, reminding listeners of the delicate alignment between compassion and caution. It is a tale that teaches the importance of empathy and the need for wisdom in protecting oneself from harm, ensuring that trust is placed where it is deserved.

La Víbora Ingrata is a powerful illustration of **Rectitude**, the final building block of sainthood. Miguel's initial compassion and generosity reflect virtues we cherish, but the story teaches a valuable lesson: True righteousness requires discernment with others. **Rectitude** calls us to act with integrity, show kindness, and recognize when to guard ourselves against betrayal. Like Miguel, we are called to use empathy with wisdom, ensuring our moral strength remains steadfast despite deception. This chapter explores how **Rectitude** anchors us, guiding our actions with resilience, vigilance, and unwavering integrity, even when our kindness is met with betrayal. **Rectitude**, like heat, bound Miguel's compassion and wisdom, demonstrating that even acts of kindness require discernment and resilience.

In connecting the tale to the theme of justice, the story of Miguel and Seraphina offers a vivid illustration of the need for discernment, justice, and ethical living—core components of **Rectitude**. Miguel's initial act of kindness in saving Seraphina reflects generosity and compassion. Yet the betrayal he suffers serves as a poignant reminder of the importance of balancing empathy with moral vigilance. This tale illustrates that true righteousness requires discernment in relationships, balancing empathy with wisdom to ensure that our actions genuinely support others without compromising our own ethical boundaries. **Rectitude**, as explored in the text, demands more than mere personal ethics—it extends to societal transformation and the pursuit of justice, echoing the call for believers to align their actions with the gospel's message of righteousness.

In Latine contexts, where cultural narratives often emphasize the dangers of misplaced trust, it symbolizes the potential for betrayal that lurks even in seemingly harmless relationships. This resonates with the understanding of **Rectitude** in Christian theology, which calls for a deeper integration of moral strength to face personal and societal challenges. Just as Miguel learns that appearances can deceive, **Rectitude** teaches us to maintain integrity, discernment, and resilience, ensuring our actions are aligned with justice like God's. Adopting the Latine tradition of storytelling and the principles of liberation theology and *misión integral* (championed by Latin American theologians Padilla and Escobar), **Rectitude** moves beyond individual morality to confront larger societal injustices, reflecting the virtue's role as heat in the spiritual diet, holding all other elements together with moral courage and justice.

As noted earlier, *misión integral*, also known as "integral mission," refers to a holistic approach to Christian mission that integrates evangelism with social action, emphasizing that the proclamation of the gospel and the demonstration of its transformative impact through justice and service are inseparable.

The concept of *misión integral* aligns deeply with the virtue of **Rectitude** as explored in the story of *La Víbora Ingrata*. Both emphasize that justice and ethical living are essential to Christian life, transcending individual acts of kindness. In *misión integral*, evangelism and social action are inseparable, much like **Rectitude** demands ethical living that addresses personal morality and societal injustice. Just as Miguel's discernment in the face of betrayal teaches a lesson about balancing compassion with wisdom, this approach to mission calls for a holistic approach to it—one that integrates the proclamation of faith with the practical pursuit of justice, echoing the Latine commitment to advocacy for the poor and people facing oppression. Both frameworks guide believers to embody justice as a transformative force in the world, ensuring that faith is lived out not just in words but through actions that confront injustice and inequality.

Rectitude must remain adaptable and compassionate, avoiding the trap of moralism. This equilibrium reflects a commitment to righteous and deeply compassionate justice, as liberation theology advocates. Genuine **Rectitude** requires alignment with justice, integrating personal integrity with advocacy for individuals from marginalized backgrounds. In Christian theology, **Rectitude** is the practice of relational justice, ethical living, and righteousness that engages societal transformation that transcends individual ethics. It calls believers to live in alignment with the gospel's mandate for justice, embodying both personal and communal responsibility. **Rectitude** is not simply an individual spiritual discipline; it demands action in daily life, standing against injustice, and advocating for those marginalized by society. This virtue invites Christians to integrate their faith with active justice through volunteering, human rights advocacy, or confronting systemic inequalities.

Where Rolheiser emphasizes personal morality, theologians like Ellacuría argue that justice must go beyond charity, demanding systemic transformation. **Rectitude**, then, requires personal integrity and a commitment to dismantling oppression. In Latine contexts, **Rectitude** is often intertwined with the principles of liberation theology and *misión integral*, emphasizing the need for justice-oriented faith that engages society. Catholic Latin American theologians like Gutiérrez, Jon Sobrino, and others argue that **Rectitude** demands a commitment to the poor and people facing oppression, echoing the biblical mandate "to act justly and to love mercy and to walk humbly with your God" (Mic. 6:8 NIV).[1] This understanding of **Rectitude** goes beyond personal morality, calling for social action that reflects God's Kingdom on earth.

Bartolomé de las Casas embodied **Rectitude** in his defense of Indigenous rights during the colonial period, demonstrating how ethical living drives justice for oppressed people.[2] Miguel Hidalgo y Costilla's fight for Mexican independence reflects the fusion of personal conviction and public leadership motivated by **Rectitude.**[3] De las Casas embodied Rectitude in his defense of Indigenous rights during the colonial period, demonstrating how ethical living drives justice for oppressed people; however, as scholars including Luis Tapia Rubio have noted, his efforts were also shaped by the broader structures of coloniality.[4]

Table 7.1 Moral and Ethical Principles in Rectitude

Virtue	Biblical Foundation	Application in Spiritual Life	Historical Example
Integrity	Proverbs 11:3	Honesty in all actions	Ignacio de Loyola's disciplined lifestyle
Justice	Micah 6:8	Commitment to fairness	Bartolomé de las Casas's advocacy for Indigenous people
Humility	Philippians 2:3–4	Living with grace and service	St. Francis of Assisi's life of poverty
Courage	Joshua 1:9	Standing for righteousness	Óscar Romero's resistance to oppression

Judy Baca embodies **Rectitude** through art and activism by blending creative expression with social justice. Renowned for large-scale public murals, her work, including *The Great Wall of Los Angeles,* highlights historical memory and the experiences of marginalized communities. Rooted in her Chicana heritage, Baca's art emphasizes community collaboration, storytelling, and cultural identity, using visual narratives to inspire societal transformation.[5] *Misión integral* grounds the biblical concept of morality by emphasizing that true righteousness (**Rectitude**) integrates right relationships with God and others, aligning personal holiness with societal justice. The idea of righteousness, often understood as living ethically and having a right relationship with God, is expanded in this view of mission to include the pursuit of justice and care for individuals from marginalized backgrounds, which are core biblical themes. In this approach, **Rectitude** is not limited to individual **Piety** but extends to actions that reflect God's concern for the people facing oppression and the needy. For example, the prophetic tradition in the Old Testament—especially in books like Amos and Isaiah—calls for righteousness through just dealings, defense of the poor, and fair treatment of others (Amos 5:24; Isa. 58:6–7). *Misión integral* takes these themes and asserts that Christian **Rectitude** must manifest both in personal spiritual transformation and in active efforts to transform society.[6]

Proponents of this, such as Padilla and Escobar, often draw on passages like Micah 6:8—which calls for justice, mercy, and humility before God—to argue that biblical **Rectitude** encompasses justice-seeking actions and spiritual devotion.[7] In the New Testament, this holistic understanding is reflected in the ministry of Jesus, who not only called people to repentance but also healed the sick, fed the hungry, and advocated for those on the margins (Luke 4:18–19). So for evangelicals, **Rectitude** is understood as aligning one's inner life and outward actions with God's will, enriching justice, compassion, and righteousness in every aspect of life.[8] Thus, **Rectitude** is the heat that binds together the virtues of **Majesty**, **Piety**, and **Solitude**, providing the moral strength to stand firm in one's convictions during trials. It equips believers to navigate the complexities of life with integrity, continually aligning their actions with justice, similarly to God's. Incorporating Latine spirituality and social activism elements, this concept becomes a dynamic force that guides personal and societal transformation.

Biblical Models of Rectitude

In the stories of Joseph in Egypt and Daniel in Babylon, we find profound biblical examples of **Rectitude**, where ethical living and justice shine in the face of societal oppression and personal trials. Joseph and Daniel lived in foreign lands under conditions of slavery and exile. Yet their steadfast commitment to just and ethical relationships as an expression of righteousness reflecting justice through right relationships in challenging contexts allowed them to navigate the challenges with grace and discernment.

Joseph, sold into slavery by his siblings, rose to a position of influence in Egypt not by compromising his values but by maintaining his integrity. Even when faced with temptation and false accusations (Gen. 39:7–20), he remained steadfast in his commitment to justice and righteousness. His ability to interpret dreams (Gen. 41:15–16) and his moral fortitude led to his eventual elevation to a place of power where he could save his people during famine (Gen. 41:39–40). Joseph's life mirrors the principle of *misión integral*—he proclaimed faith in God. He demonstrated its transformative impact through his leadership, bringing spiritual and physical deliverance to his family and the nation of Egypt (Gen. 45:5–7).

Similarly, Daniel, living in Babylon during the exile, remained resolute in his faith, refusing to compromise his spiritual beliefs, even when threatened with death (Dan. 6:10). His dedication to justice, combined with his wisdom and courage, allowed him to influence the kings of Babylon while staying true to his convictions (Dan. 1:8; 6:4). Daniel's life reflects **Rectitude** by showing how one can remain morally upright in a foreign land, advocating for justice and righteousness in the face of oppression. Like Joseph, Daniel's story highlights the importance of maintaining integrity, even when society's pressures tempt us to stray from our values.

Both Joseph and Daniel demonstrate how **Rectitude** is not merely an internal or personal virtue but one that has the power to transform societies. In their respective contexts of slavery and exile, their commitment to justice and ethical living positioned them as agents of change, embodying the essence of *misión integral*—where faith and social action converge. Through their stories, we see how maintaining **Rectitude** enables individuals to survive adversity and become catalysts for justice, aligning personal righteousness with the greater good of society.

Rectitude in the Life of Jesus

As the ultimate model of **Rectitude**, Jesus Christ embodied and demonstrated how to love others with unwavering integrity, justice, and righteousness. Throughout his ministry, Jesus used the theological foundations of spiritual life to craft a path of love that his followers are called to emulate. Jesus carefully blended these elements into a perfect "diet" for living a life of service, compassion, and moral strength, showing us how to love God and others without compromise.

In the New Testament, the Zealots exemplified **Rectitude**'s steward of justice-like qualities—strength, courage, and integrity—in their struggle for justice. Their zeal for righteousness parallels the heat of **Rectitude**, which binds and fuels a life dedicated to social transformation. Jesus's understanding of **Rectitude** emphasized relational justice, grounded in the right relationships that transform personal virtue into societal action. He consistently stood up for individuals from marginalized backgrounds and confronted ingrained injustices, demonstrating that love must be rooted in ethical living. One profound example of Jesus practicing **Rectitude** is his cleansing of the temple, where he drove out the money changers exploiting worshippers (Matt. 21:12–13). Jesus consistently challenged hypocrisy—especially within religious institutions—demonstrating that **Rectitude** involves the boldness to expose duplicity and uphold justice.

Moreover, Jesus's teachings in the Sermon on the Mount reveal his deep commitment to ethical living. He expanded on the meaning of righteousness, urging his followers to go beyond superficial adherence to the law and instead cultivate hearts of justice and compassion. In Matthew 5:20, Jesus declared, "For I tell you, unless your righteousness exceeds that of the scribes and Pharisees, you will never enter the kingdom of heaven." In this, he calls his followers to a higher standard of integrity—one that seeks true justice, mercy, and love for others.

Jesus consistently ministered to others by embodying **Rectitude**—loving without compromise while addressing their spiritual and physical needs. In his interaction with the Samaritan woman at the well (John 4:1–26), Jesus demonstrated a radical form of love, breaking societal norms and barriers to extend grace and truth. In this story, he both loved and corrected, offering the woman living water while addressing the brokenness in her life. His ability to stabilize love, truth, and justice in every interaction reflects the heart of **Rectitude**: offering compassion while remaining steadfast in righteousness.

Another example of Jesus's use of **Rectitude** in ministry is his response to the woman caught in adultery (John 8:3–11 NIV). The Pharisees sought to trap Jesus into condemning her, but instead, he displayed perfect ethical living. He neither condoned her sin nor unjustly condemned her. His words "Let anyone among you who is without sin be the first to throw a stone at her" and his final command, "Go now and leave your life of sin," demonstrate how Jesus combines justice with mercy, embodying the fullness of **Rectitude** in his interactions.

Jesus's followers saw him embodying ethical living, justice, and love. The apostles and early church leaders understood that Jesus's teachings were grounded in the principle of **Rectitude** and sought to follow his example. In 1 Peter 2:22–23, Peter writes of Jesus, "He committed no sin, and no deceit was found in his mouth. When they hurled their insults at him, he did not retaliate; when he suffered, he made no threats. Instead, he entrusted himself to him who judges justly." This passage emphasizes that Jesus maintained his righteousness and ethical living even in the face of injustice, serving as the perfect example of **Rectitude** for his followers.

The apostle Paul also reflected on Jesus's life as a model of righteous living. In Philippians 2:5–8, Paul exhorts believers to "have the same mindset as Christ Jesus," who humbled himself despite his authority and became obedient to death on the cross. This obedience to God's will, even at high personal cost, highlights the ultimate example of **Rectitude**—living entirely with God's justice and love, even when it requires self-sacrifice. Throughout his ministry, Jesus demonstrated how to blend the spiritual and theological foundations of **MPSR** into a life that reflects God's love and justice. He showed that love, to be accurate, must be grounded in righteousness and that ethical living is essential for transforming the world. Like a master chef, Jesus carefully prepared a "diet" for spiritual nourishment that his followers can live by, harmonizing love with justice and compassion with truth.

Jesus is the ultimate example of building a proportional spiritual life. His life and teachings show us that sainthood—represented through **MPSR**—is not an abstract or unattainable ideal. Instead, it is a practical, lived experience that transforms both individuals and communities through the power of love grounded in righteousness. Just as Jesus blended these elements perfectly in his own life, we are called to follow his example, integrating these theological foundations to craft a spiritual life that is nourishing, transformative, and deeply rooted in the love and justice of God.

Ignacio Loyola and Rectitude

Like that of a warrior tempered by heat, Ignacio de Loyola's life reflects how **Rectitude** binds strength, discipline, and integrity. His Spiritual Exercises not only crafted a protector of truth for God but instilled in them a commitment to justice that resonates within the Latine community's pursuit of righteousness amid systemic challenges. His pilgrimage, marked by his "cannon experience" and formulation of the Spiritual Exercises, provides a model of how profound personal transformation can lead to widespread spiritual renewal.

Ignacio was a mystic who loved God exceptionally, surpassing even what one might expect from a saint. He wasn't a renowned scholar like Augustine or Thomas Aquinas, nor was he a martyr like Peter or Paul, and he never reached the literary fame of Teresa of Ávila or Benedict, nor was he as widely cherished as Francis or Thérèse of Lisieux. Yet what truly distinguished him was the depth of his devotion to God and his love for the world—two pursuits in which he excelled in a singular, heartfelt way.[9] Ignacio's life demonstrates that **Rectitude** is not merely individual but is meant to transform societies and structures, much like the reforms he pioneered in the sixteenth century, which continue to influence spiritual practices five hundred years later. Through my spiritual accompaniment with Nora Beatriz Kviatkovski, an Ignatian scholar deeply devoted to the spirituality of the Religious of Jesus and Mary, I have been able to experience Ignacio profoundly.

He was born in 1491 to a noble family in the Basque region of Spain; Ignacio's early life was marked by ambition, a desire for military glory, and service to the Spanish crown. His life, however, took a dramatic turn in 1521 when a cannonball severely wounded him during the Battle of Pamplona. His recovery marked the beginning of a profound spiritual transformation.[10] During his recovery, Ignacio had access to a book on Christ's and saints' lives. In this period of reading and reflection, he began to question his previous life and started contemplating a life of spiritual commitment.

The "cannon experience," as this moment of injury and transformation is often called, catalyzed Ignacio's conversion.[11] He famously said during this time, "What if I should do what Saint Francis or Dominic did?" This marked his first steps toward radical spiritual reform, choosing the path of ethical living, righteousness, and justice over his former pursuits of worldly success. This was his embrace of **Rectitude**, as he shifted from serving the temporal powers of the world to dedicating his life to the eternal power of God. True righteousness involves upholding ethical integrity in our interactions, which are just and grounded relationships with others, aiming to support fairness, accountability, and mutual respect.

After his recovery, Ignacio laid down his sword at the shrine of Montserrat and dedicated himself to God's service. This symbolic act of renouncing his former life as a soldier signaled the beginning of his pilgrimage to become a "spiritual warrior" for God. His conversion reflects **Rectitude** in action—turning away from a life driven by self-interest and ambition toward one dedicated to ethical living and justice.[12]

His most enduring contribution to Christian spirituality is *The Spiritual Exercises*, a structured series of meditations, prayers, and reflections designed to help individuals cultivate their relationship with God. These exercises embody **Rectitude** by guiding individuals to align their will with God's and to develop ethical living that translates into just actions in the world. Ignacio crafted these exercises for years, drawing from his personal experiences of spiritual struggle and growth.

The *Principle and Foundation*, the opening meditation of Ignacio de Loyola's *Spiritual Exercises*, establishes the purpose of human life as "to praise, reverence, and serve God." This core teaching embodies *Rectitude*, calling individuals to align their entire being with God's actions in the world. Ignacio emphasizes that all Creation exists to help people grow closer to God, and true spiritual discernment requires using these gifts wisely while remaining detached from anything that hinders this purpose. The foundation of *The Spiritual Exercises* shapes the path of moral and spiritual growth, ensuring that every action reflects a higher calling toward God's glory.

As the exercises progress, participants are led through self-examination, the discernment of spirits, and the imitation of Christ, particularly his commitment to justice and love for individuals from marginalized backgrounds.

One of his most famous sayings, "To give and not to count the cost," encapsulates this deep sense of service rooted in ethical living.[13]

The exercises follow a structured progression that includes the First Week, focusing on self-awareness and sin, and the Second Week, which centers on the life of Christ and the choice to follow him. The final weeks lead individuals into the passion of Christ and, ultimately, into a deeper relationship with God's justice. In "The Contemplation to Attain Love," the final meditation of *The Spiritual Exercises*, Ignacio de Loyola calls individuals to recognize all Creation as a gift from God, meant to lead them back to him. This reflection cultivates love for God, emphasizing that true love is expressed in deeds rather than words. Ignacio teaches that just as God's love is revealed through his gifts—granting being to elements, life to plants, sensation to animals, and intelligence to humans—people are called to respond through gratitude, service, and ethical living. This contemplation reinforces **Rectitude**, guiding individuals to align their lives with God's greater glory through justice and devotion.

These exercises embody a process of articulation, integration, and collaboration. Ignacio articulated a clear vision of spiritual and ethical living, integrated it into a structured practice, and then shared it widely, collaborating with others to spread this method of spiritual formation. The exercises are still used today, a testament to their transformative power. More than five hundred years after their inception, their longevity demonstrates how the principle of **Rectitude**, when properly cultivated, provides lasting spiritual nourishment.

Ignacio de Loyola's life and work were revolutionary in their time. During the Reformation, when the Catholic Church faced significant internal and external challenges, Ignacio's vision for spiritual renewal was a bold and transformative response. His formation of the Jesuit order in 1540,[14] sanctioned by Pope Paul III, directly resulted from his belief that spiritual and moral reform was necessary for the church's survival and growth. The Jesuits became known for their rigorous education, commitment to social justice, and missionary work—further exemplifying the idea that **Rectitude**, when practiced collectively, can reform individuals and entire societies.

The quote "Go forth and set the world on fire," commonly attributed to Ignacio though not found verbatim in his extant letters, epitomizes his belief that true spiritual reform must lead to action.[15] His vision for reform

Table 7.2 Ignacio de Loyola's Weeks and Rectitude

Week	Focus	Impact on Rectitude
First Week	Self-examination and awareness of sin	Leads to ethical living by promoting self-awareness, recognition of personal failings, and a desire to align my relationships with God's will
Second Week	Life of Christ, call to follow him	Promotes justice and righteousness by encouraging the imitation of Christ, especially in service to others and moral decisions
Third Week	Passion of Christ and suffering	Strengthens perseverance in righteousness by contemplating Christ's suffering and developing compassion and moral courage
Fourth Week	Resurrection, cultivating love for Christ and commitment	Seeks a commitment to living a just and ethical life rooted in love and gratitude for Christ's resurrection and redemption

was spiritual and practical; he believed ethical living should lead to societal transformation. The Jesuit motto, *ad majorem Dei gloriam* ("For the Greater Glory of God"), reflects this holistic understanding of **Rectitude**, where all actions are directed toward glorifying God through just and righteous living.[16]

In *The Spiritual Exercises*, each week plays a crucial role in shaping the virtue of **Rectitude** by guiding individuals through spiritual growth. The first week encourages self-examination and awareness of sin, prompting a desire to align one's life with God's will. The second week encourages imitation of Christ and cultivates one's commitment to justice and moral decisions in daily life. The third week focuses on Christ's passion, cultivating compassion and perseverance in righteousness, even suffering. Finally, the fourth week celebrates the resurrection, inspiring a life of love, gratitude, and ethical commitment to justice. This structured pilgrimage strengthens personal integrity and equips individuals to act justly in the world, making **Rectitude** a central element in their spiritual nourishment.

Ignacio de Loyola's legacy is evident in the continuing relevance of the Spiritual Exercises and the Jesuit order's influence on education, social justice, and spiritual formation. Jesuit schools and universities worldwide continue to emphasize the integration of faith and justice, demonstrating how the principle of **Rectitude**, as articulated by him, remains a foundational element of Jesuit spirituality. These exercises are still practiced by individuals and communities seeking to cultivate their spiritual lives and align their actions with God's will. The structure of the exercises, which blends contemplation with action, reflects the core tenets of **Rectitude**—ethical living, justice, and righteousness. His vision for a world transformed by individuals living out these values inspires people today, just as it did five hundred years ago.

A Building Block for Sustenance Spirituality

Rectitude, as explored throughout this text, stands at the core of sustaining a rich and nourishing spiritual life. It calls us to live with ethical living, justice, and righteousness in personal and communal contexts. Ignacio de Loyola demonstrated this through the Spiritual Exercises, where spiritual nourishment requires consistent self-examination, alignment with God's will, and action that flows from deep contemplation. But how does this virtue translate into a spiritual "diet" that can sustain us daily, especially within the Latin American theological context?

The rich heritage of Latin American theologians, activists, and thinkers provides profound insights into how **Rectitude** can be applied as a source of sustenance in our spiritual lives. Figures such as Bartolomé de las Casas and Miguel Hidalgo y Costilla embody **Rectitude** through their commitment to justice, challenging oppressive systems, and advocating for individuals from marginalized backgrounds.[17] As Lewis Hanke highlights in his work on de las Casas, the friar's lifelong defense of Indigenous rights was rooted in a deep sense of ethical living and justice, aligning with the spiritual foundation of **Rectitude**. In the same way,[18] Miguel Hidalgo's fight for Mexican independence, as described by Michael C. Meyer and William H. Beezley, illustrates how personal conviction can lead to broad societal change when guided by ethical principles.[19]

To translate **Rectitude** into a diet for spiritual nourishment, we must first understand that it is not merely a call to personal morality but a deeply embedded responsibility to act in the world. Luis Pérez Aguirre emphasizes this point, noting that proper spiritual growth is inseparable from justice, especially in contexts where oppression persists.[20] His reflections serve as a guide for integrating justice-oriented living into everyday spiritual practices. Camilo Maccise, in *En el invierno eclesial*, further underscores the importance of personal transformation leading to social transformation.[21] Maccise's work teaches that personal holiness must feed into collective action, a spirituality that is both sustainable and impactful in addressing the world's injustices. Pedro Bonifacio Palacios (Almafuerte), a renowned Argentine poet, adds to this conversation by focusing on resilience and moral strength. Almafuerte's works often reflect the necessity of standing firm in one's principles, even when facing significant opposition. His poetry encourages a deep internal fortitude, essential for maintaining **Rectitude** in challenging circumstances. This fortitude is a crucial ingredient in a spiritual diet, ensuring that individuals remain committed to justice and integrity even when the road is difficult.

Through her art and social activism, Judy Baca shows us another way to integrate **Rectitude** into our lives. Her work, as discussed by Shifra Goldman, demonstrates how creative expression can be a form of justice and moral advocacy.[22] Baca's murals, which give voice to marginalized communities, embody the principles of **Rectitude** by merging artistic vision with a call to action. This integration of creative expression and ethical living highlights how diverse practices can form part of a nourishing spiritual life, where justice and art coexist to elevate the human spirit.

The spiritual diet that sustains our faith must also be forward-looking. Dietrich Bonhoeffer (who was murdered by the Nazis) and Jon Sobrino (whom the church criticized for emphasizing Jesus's humanity in a way that potentially neglected Christ's divinity) provide critical frameworks for this. Bonhoeffer's *Ethics* articulates how living a life of moral courage and ethical rigor is not optional for Christians but foundational to following Christ.[23] His reflections remind us that a spiritual life must be built on a solid foundation of justice and moral action. Similarly, Sobrino, in *Jesus the Liberator*, invites us to see **Rectitude** not just as a personal virtue but as a communal practice deeply embedded in the pursuit of justice for the poor and people facing oppression.[24]

We must learn from these thinkers to craft a spiritual diet that nourishes and sustains. A healthy spiritual life requires stability of self-reflection, community engagement, creative expression, and action rooted in justice. In this sense, **Rectitude** is the heat that holds all other spiritual practices together, ensuring that they lead not only to personal growth but also to the transformation of society.

To apply Rectitude in your own spiritual life, consider these steps:

1. **Daily reflection:** Like in the First Week of the Spiritual Exercises, practice daily self-examination. Reflect on how your actions align with your moral values and commitment to justice. Incorporate prayers that ask for discernment and the courage to act with integrity.
2. **Community engagement:** Learn from figures like de las Casas and Miguel Hidalgo by becoming involved in community efforts for justice. Whether through advocacy, volunteering, or supporting marginalized voices, ensure that your spirituality leads to action.
3. **Creative expression:** Follow Judy Baca's example by integrating your creative talents into your spiritual life. Whether through art, writing, or music, use your gifts to promote justice and bring dialogue about ethical living.
4. **Endurance in justice:** Draw on the resilience reflected in Almafuerte's poetry and Bonhoeffer's writings. Stand firm in your commitment to justice, even when faced with adversity, trusting that your spiritual diet will sustain you through challenges.
5. **Collaboration:** Finally, integrate the wisdom of others into your spiritual pilgrimage. Look to theologians like Sobrino, Maccise, and Romero, who emphasize collaboration in pursuing justice as you seek to build a holistic and nourishing spiritual life.

When woven into the fabric of our spiritual practices, **Rectitude** provides sustenance that enables personal transformation and societal change. In Romero's words, the pilgrimage toward justice is ongoing and requires aligning ourselves with God's will through love, courage, and righteousness.

The Integral Role of the Theological Foundations in a Nourishing Spiritual Diet

The elements of **MPSR**, when intertwined in the spiritual life, offer a comprehensive framework for understanding the spiritual diet necessary for transformation. Each building block contributes essential nourishment for personal growth and societal impact, reinforcing one another in cultivating a faith and justice cycle. **Rectitude**, representing ethical living and justice, forms the foundational backbone of this nourishment, guiding the believer to live with strength and resilience in the face of life's challenges. **Majesty** calls us to govern with authority, **Piety** allows us to intercede and cultivates our looking for God, and **Solitude** teaches us vulnerability and reflection. Together, they create a spiritual diet that nourishes the whole person—cognitively, emotionally, and spiritually. By taking on these blocks, much like a skilled chef preparing a well-rounded meal, believers can cultivate a spirituality that sustains personal holiness and meaningfully engages with the world.

Like heat in cooking, **Rectitude** is the force that binds all elements of a spiritual life. It provides moral intensity and courage, ensuring our beliefs align with our actions and that our spirituality extends from personal growth into societal transformation. **Rectitude**, emphasizing ethical living, justice, and righteousness, is the key to maintaining a cohesive and nourishing spiritual life. It offers a guiding framework that aligns our inner values with our outward actions, ensuring that our emotions and spiritual practices are grounded in ethical clarity. Emotionally, **Rectitude** strengthens inner peace by aligning our actions with our principles, reducing the internal conflict that arises when we act contrary to our beliefs. Spiritually, it cultivates our link with God as we live out God's call for justice, righteousness, and compassion.

Rectitude bridges emotional responses and spiritual wisdom, transforming feelings like frustration or empathy into actions that reflect God's will. In Latin American theology, this commitment to justice is known as *compromiso*—a deep sense of solidarity with the marginalized that turns personal conviction into meaningful social change. Rooted in the Christian obligation to challenge oppression and promote equity, committing to justice aligns faith with practical engagement, exemplified in the work of liberation theologians who integrate justice and spirituality in both personal and communal life. As the foundation of a spiritually nourishing life, **Rectitude** helps us integrate our emotions and spirituality, guiding us to live with personal growth and societal transformation. Through **Rectitude**, we embody a spirituality that is not only transformative but deeply rooted in justice, compassion, and love.

Drawing from Latine traditions, which emphasize resilience, communal strength, and justice, we find rich examples of how these spiritual, theological foundations are not merely theoretical but are deeply embedded in the lived experiences of individuals and communities. Integrating these values with practices like *misión integral* and liberation theology further enriches the spiritual diet by ensuring that faith and action are inseparable. The wisdom of theologians such as Ignacio de Loyola and Gutiérrez and figures like de las Casas and Hidalgo reminds us that robust spiritual nourishment requires personal transformation and societal engagement. The interconnectedness of **MPSR** offers a transformative path for those seeking spiritual growth. Just as Latine culture combines diverse elements to create a rich and nourishing identity, these spiritual principles create a robust spiritual diet that cultivates personal and communal justice.

Rectitude as the Ethical Backbone of Transformative Faith

Rectitude is the ethical anchor, ensuring that faith transcends private belief and becomes a public witness rooted in integrity, justice, and moral courage. The **MPSR** framework transforms spiritual conviction into ethical action, compelling believers to align themselves with righteousness, justice, and the common good. Without **Rectitude**, faith risks hypocrisy and passivity, while its inclusion engenders personal renewal and the restoration of society.

Rectitude is not limited to avoiding wrongdoing but encompasses actively pursuing what is right. It embodies the biblical call to justice, wherein faith is measured not by ritual alone but by equity, honesty, and advocacy for the vulnerable. Absent ethical responsibility, spirituality becomes incomplete, ignoring the inseparable nature of holiness and justice. **Rectitude** thus ensures that reverence for God translates into just relationships, principled decisions, and an unwavering commitment to truth. Practically, **Rectitude** emerges in everyday actions, communal engagement, and the boldness to confront societal injustices. In Latine traditions, it resonates with historical struggles for liberation and human dignity, emphasizing faith's integral role in promoting equality. Beyond personal righteousness, **Rectitude** demands solidarity with the oppressed, wisdom in moral dilemmas, and the integrity to uphold justice, even at high personal cost—guarding against spiritual stagnation by grounding faith in tangible, embodied practice.

When **Rectitude** is lacking, religion can become self-serving, detached from injustice, and indifferent to suffering—"rich in religious language but hollow in ethical substance." Yet an overemphasis on **Rectitude** absent of

Majesty, **Piety**, and **Solitude** risks self-righteousness. Genuine **Rectitude** unites moral clarity with compassion, ensuring that the pursuit of justice remains anchored in humility and recognition of every person's dignity.

Rectitude bridges belief and action in the broader theological and social context, ensuring faith remains active, restorative, and ethically responsible. This chapter has shown that **Rectitude** is not mere rule following but rather the embodiment of Kingdom values—love, justice, and righteousness—that shape individual character and communal responsibility.

Ultimately, **Rectitude** is the spiritual backbone vital for an authentic, transformative faith. It integrates spirituality, compelling believers to go beyond prayer and contemplation toward ethical action, communal accountability, and a dedicated pursuit of justice. In the next chapter, these four virtues unite to create a holistic, dynamic spirituality, equipping believers for a life of depth, integrity, and purpose—urgently needed in our world.

Part Three

Cultivating the Sacred Banquet

The doors to the world of the wild Self are few but precious.
If you have a deep scar, that is a door, if you have an old, old story, that is a door.
If you love the sky and the water so much you almost cannot bear it, that is a door.
If you yearn for a deeper life, a full life, a sane life, that is a door.

—Clarissa Pinkola Estés

Chapter Eight

Noble Majesty, Sacred Piety, Vulnerable Solitude, and Just Rectitude

The Condition for membership in God's project is accepting Yahweh as the true God and commitment to respond faithfully to this faithful God.

—María Pilar Aquino

To start this chapter, I invite you to know the Yaqui *cuento* of "El chapulín brujo."[1] Mauricio, a poor youth gathering firewood, meets a powerful *brujo* (sorcerer) who offers secret knowledge for the price of his soul. Desperate, he agrees and is transformed into a grasshopper (*chapulín*) with prodigious power. This marvel soon became a curse: An insatiable appetite drives the *chapulín* to devour field and village alike. Fear and remorse break through the hunger when the sorcerer confronts the rampaging creature. Mauricio begs for mercy, and the *brujo* restores his human form, leaving him with the hard-won insight that gifts unmoored from virtue destroy both bearer and community.

The *cuento* offers three truths on our pilgrimage for saintly art. First, ambition is never neutral; it serves or consumes the common good. Second, every power must be held within the bounds of mindfulness and responsibility. Third, actual change is possible when contrition meets grace. Like Mauricio, each saint faces similar bargains—temptations to trade integrity for influence, contentment for excess. Therefore, the tale becomes a mirror, exposing where our hungers outpace our wisdom and calling us to realign desire with justice (this challenges us to actively incorporate **MPSR** into our spiritual practices). Opening the chapter with this story is an invitation to live God's mission boldly: to fuse noble ambition with just rectitude and to practice habits that nourish soul and neighbor.

The Role of Context

Laura Esquivel's novel—and Alfonso Arau's screen adaptation—*Like Water for Chocolate* (*Como agua para chocolate*, 1992) tells of Tita, whose unspoken love is poured into her cooking during the turmoil of the Mexican Revolution. In Spanish, the title describes water brought just to a boil for making hot chocolate; likewise, the film treats food as manifest emotion, a conduit through which hidden longings erupt in tangible form. Every dish Tita prepares transmits her passion or grief to those who eat it, revealing how the ordinary can become sacramental in the right hands.

The story's culinary spirituality offers a living parable for this chapter as a "spiritual diet." **Majesty** is tasted whenever Tita's work draws family and strangers into awed silence before a reality larger than themselves. **Piety** appears in the careful rituals of the kitchen and table, each recipe rehearsing devotion through habit. **Solitude** surfaces in the young woman's enforced seclusion; within those lonely hours, she discovers the ferment of prayerful self-examination. Finally, **Rectitude** breaks through whenever Tita, defying oppressive customs, chooses truth over convenience—her meals become protests seasoned with moral courage. One narrative enfolds all four theological foundations.

Notice how the setting shapes the menu: Revolution, patriarchal norms, and desert scarcity influence which ingredients are available and how they are shared. The starting point of all true theology is the historical reality of the oppressed, because it is there that God's saving will be disclosed and demanded.[2] Tita's cuisine, therefore, reminds us that spiritual nourishment is never abstract; it must be cooked within concrete histories and served at real tables. In the same way, each believer's "diet" must honor local culture, memory, and struggle if it hopes to satisfy genuine hunger. Like Tita's kitchen, Daniel's Babylonian diet shows that holiness is cooked within history: "Daniel resolved that he would not defile himself with the king's food, or with the wine that he drank," choosing fidelity even while serving a foreign court (Dan. 1:8 ESV).

Therefore, a nourishing "spiritual diet" balances the content of faith and its core convictions that do not change with the context that always does. Latine theologians insist on reading the two together. Ada María Isasi-Díaz calls hospitality a sacrament of mutual belonging, especially for the marginalized; it is not a courtesy but "a sanctuary with doors flung open."[3] Orlando Espín shows how popular Catholicism turns that hospitality into communal practice—pilgrimage, fiesta, devotion to local saints—so that worship is unmistakably public and political.[4] María Pilar Aquino adds that theology must be hospitable, listening first to the cries of the poor before it dares to speak. Finally, Fernando Segovia urges an intercultural method that subjects every Scripture reading to the wisdom of other cultures.[5] Scripture stays the same, but we see more when more people hold a lamp.

Latine authors help us appreciate the four spiritual elements that frame *Art of Sainthood*. Isasi-Díaz's radical welcome becomes an act of **Majesty** because she receives the stranger in God's image. **Piety**, says Espín, grows sturdy when devotion is shared bread rather than private piety. **Solitude**, treasured in Latine contemplative traditions, is the inner room where anguish and joy can be laid bare before God; it protects vitality so that outer service does not burn out. **Rectitude**, Aquino stresses, is justice enacted—truth told in public policy, wages, and borders, not only in prayer closets.[6] When the elements of **MPSR** are braided this way, content keeps its shape and context keeps its relevance. Content without the optic of the poor petrifies into ideology; context without the norm of the gospel dissolves into relativism. Liberation is their dialectical embrace.[7]

Interdependence and Faith Development

Latine theology likewise centers on interdependence. Clarissa Pinkola Estés retells folk stories in which a person's healing is never private; the heroine's restored heart becomes the village's restored future.[8] Her insight echoes Espín's: Spirituality is "profoundly communal." Ellacuría pushes the point further, arguing that reality is a history to be transformed or liberated, not merely described.[9] Joseph's rise in Egypt narrates that very transformation: Having interpreted Pharaoh's dream, he organizes grain stores "so that the land may not perish through the famine" (Gen. 41:36 ESV). If faith does not become historical praxis that liberates, it is no more than idle contemplation.[10]

Put together, these scholars insist that discipleship is inward and outward, solitary and social—one breath in, one breath out. Faith development is like the rhythm of homeostasis: The body of Christ, like any living body, corrects toward balance. **Majesty** without hospitality becomes authoritarian; **Piety** without justice becomes performance; **Solitude** without community becomes escapism; **Rectitude** without contemplation becomes exhausted activism. The disciplines must cross-pollinate.

In this model, each element of **MPSR** adds a distinctive *flavor* to Christian formation:

- **Majesty**: Honoring God's rule in every action, like *salt*, grounds and unifies all other practices.
- **Piety**: Daily devotion and compassionate service, like *fat*, enrich and sustain our faith.
- **Solitude**: Quiet attentiveness cuts through distraction, like *acid*, and sharpens spiritual perception.
- **Rectitude**: Disciplined justice in relationships and deeds, like *heat*, fuses convictions into tangible good.

These four flavors supply the labels that appear in the quadrant diagram. The four spiritual elements can then be visually represented as quadrants on a graph. Along the *x*-axis—running left to right—is a continuum of how individuals and communities experience God's presence, from apophatic stillness to kataphatic articulation (see Figure 8.1). Since at least the sixth century, Christians have described this difference using the terms *apophatic* (for the leftmost end of the spectrum) and *kataphatic* (for the rightmost end). Apophatic spirituality focuses on how God is beyond comprehension and human categories. By contrast, the kataphatic tradition accents how God can be known and experienced in the created order and seeks to draw out parallels between the created world and what is unseen.

A *y*-axis—running vertically—illustrates how humans mentally engage with God (see Figure 8.2). This creates a spectrum from epistemological

Figure 8.1 Experiencing God: The Apophatic ↔ Kataphatic Continuum (*X*-Axis)

(cognitive thinking and reasoning) connections at the top of the axis to affective (emotional) connections at the bottom.

The crossing yields our four spiritual "flavors" that Jesus himself embodies (see Figure 8.3). Here, truth lovers confront idols as prophets once did: They write, expose, and guard the holy with reverent arguments. Begin in the upper-left quadrant, where apophatic (transcendent) meets cognitive. This is the just flavor: a quiet, discerning righteousness that sifts motives the way the prophets weighed Israel's heart. Shift to the upper-right quadrant—kataphatic

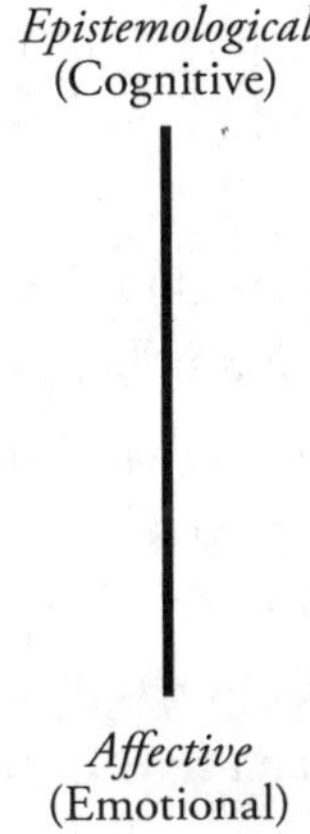

Figure 8.2 Engaging God: The Epistemological ↕ Affective Spectrum (*Y*-Axis)

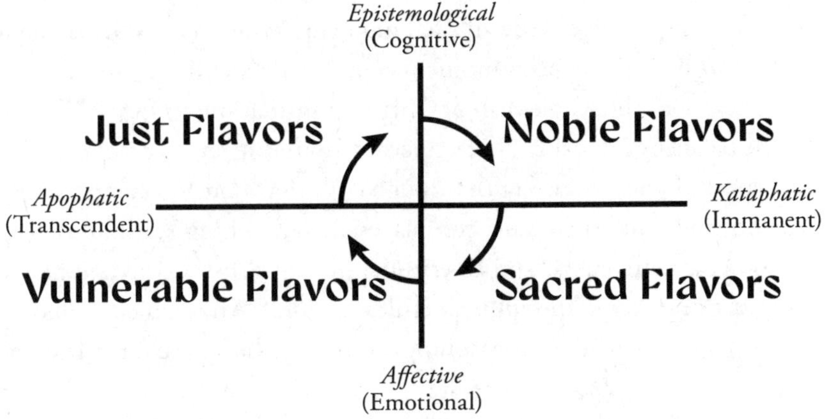

Figure 8.3 The Flavors and the Quadrants

and cognitive. Here blooms the noble flavor: clear-sighted zeal that, like Jesus cleansing the Temple, marshals intellect and will to defend God's honor. Drop to the lower-left quadrant, where apophatic intersects affective. This is the vulnerable flavor: the lamenting, desert-dwelling posture of the Essenes or of Jesus in Gethsemane, trusting that silence and tears can teach what words obscure. Finally, the lower-right quadrant unites kataphatic with affective to reveal the sacred flavor: richly emotive worship that lets passion blaze in song, procession, or prophetic protest, celebrating the nearness of God. Like the Sermon on the Mount, this quadrant reads, teaches, organizes, and even administers mercy so that neighbor and nation taste God's justice.

The matrix (a square bisected by two axes) insists that no quadrant is sufficient for a robust spirituality. The crucified peoples of history are the concrete verification that any spirituality that ignores justice is an accomplice to crucifixion.[11] Just flavors without noble flavors become brittle orthodoxy; noble flavors without just flavors dissolve into sentiment. Sacredness fades into fanaticism when it forgets vulnerable humility, and a vulnerable flavor lapses into escapism when it never rises to sacred courage. Mature saints cycle through all four: head and heart, mystery and embodiment, held in dynamic tension. By naming each flavor, the diagram in Figure 8.3 offers a diagnostic tool for churches and individuals: Where do we overindulge? Which flavor must we learn to cook with next? The goal is not bland balance but a richly layered feast where each quadrant seasons the others.

The four quadrant flavors (just, noble, vulnerable, sacred) describe *how* a community experiences God in each moment, while the **MPSR** elements explain *what* energizes those moments. In Nosrat's culinary terms, each element "seasons" the whole dish of Christian formation: **Majesty**, like salt, wakes the palate by honoring God's rule and grounding every practice; **Piety**, like fat, enriches and sustains faith through daily devotion and compassionate service; **Solitude**, like acid, cuts complacency, sharpening spiritual perception in quiet attentiveness; and **Rectitude**, like heat, fuses convictions into tangible justice through disciplined, ethical action.[12] Any element alone can overwhelm, but when all four seasonings come together, the church becomes a banquet—an anticipatory foretaste of John's vision in Revelation 5:9–13, where "every tribe and language and people and nation" lift a single song to the Lamb. Just as salt, fat, acid, and heat combine to balance a dish, **MPSR** mingle to harmonize the diverse voices of God's people into a unified, multilingual chorus of praise.

Keeping the Body of Christ in Movement

Long before Christianity, the Eleusinian Mysteries led Greek pilgrims through darkness, silence, and sudden light to reenact Demeter's loss and Persephone's return. Initiates emerged saying only, "I have seen." The rite taught that salvation is felt first in the body—through grain, torch, and song—before the mind explains it.[13]

The early Church Fathers kept that pattern but changed the plot. Cyril of Jerusalem calls baptism a mystagogy—a guided entry into secrets disclosed only after the body had passed through water and oil.[14] "Having put off the old man," he tells the newly washed, "you are now Christ-bearers." Ambrose of Milan speaks likewise: The catechumen first acts out the gospel in font and anointing; only then does the bishop unveil its meaning in nightly sermons. Experience precedes exposition so that doctrine rises from memory, not abstraction.[15]

Ignatius of Antioch, Augustine, and John Chrysostom echo the same pedagogy: Liturgy does not illustrate a lesson—it is the lesson, and the explanatory words that follow merely name what the body already knows.[16] The sequence—symbol, then speech—guards theology from disembodied speculation by rooting it in the senses.

Modern physiology refers to what the ancients intuited as homeostasis, the continual correction by which a living body stays alive.[17] In spirituality, the four foundations play that regulatory role. **Majesty** calls the church to look up in worship; **Rectitude** pulls it back to earth in justice. **Piety** preserves memory through ritual; **Solitude** clears clogged spiritual arteries by silence and fasting. When any element dominates, the body drifts toward pathology: **Majestic** awe without **Rectitude** breeds tyranny; **Rectitude** without **Piety** forgets why it fights; **Piety** without **Solitude** hardens into routine; **Solitude** without **Majesty** evaporates into self-absorption.

Mystagogy supplies the corrective mechanism. Because the sacraments continually reenact the gospel in miniature, they recalibrate the four foundations every time they are celebrated. At the Last Supper, Jesus embodies that corrective rhythm, washing his disciples' feet and commanding, "I have given you an example, that you also should do just as I have done to you" (John 13:14–15 ESV), so that table fellowship pivots seamlessly into justice-shaped service. *Liturgy becomes a dangerous memory*: It subverts every order that crucifies and calls the Church to historical effectiveness.[18] Consider the communion: The preface lifts hearts in **Majesty**, the anamnesis rehearses **Piety**, the kneeling quiet invites **Solitude**, and the dismissal—"Go in peace to love and serve"—propels **Rectitude**. One rite, four pulses, perfect balance.

Cyril of Jerusalem's sentence dismantles every false divide between matter and mystery: "The body is washed with water, the soul by the Spirit; the body is anointed with oil, the mind with grace. What you enact outwardly, God perfects within."[19] It announces that grace rides tangible signs like breath carries life to blood. The four foundations realign whenever a rite is celebrated—baptism, communion, and so on. **Majesty** lifts the heart in praise; **Piety** recalls the saving story; **Solitude** opens a pocket of hush where the soul can listen; **Rectitude** sends the assembly out to heal what is broken. Then sacrament (spiritual practices) is the church's built-in reflex for homeostasis: Culture may tug disciples toward triumphalism, activism, ritualism, or escapism, but the liturgy pulls them back to center until understanding catches up with embodiment. When saints yoke ancient mystagogy to the modern language of homeostasis, they ensure steady and alive formation—always self-correcting, never static—until, as Paul says, "Christ is formed in you" (Gal. 4:19 ESV). Galatians 4:19 ends with a plural "you"—more like a Texas "y'all" than an individual "you"—reminding us that Paul's longing is for Christ to be formed in each believer and the whole community.

A Seat at the Scroll Table

John's vision in Revelation 5 opens with a sealed scroll clenched in the right hand of the One on the throne. A hush falls—no heavenly or earthly creature can break the wax. Then the Lamb appears, "standing as though slain," and heaven erupts. The scene is more than celestial pageantry; it is liturgy in technicolor. **Majesty** resounds in the thunder of "Worthy!" as elders fling crowns before the throne. **Piety** is audible in the four living creatures chanting an ancient creed: Creation exists for God's delight. **Solitude** slips in when John weeps alone, his tears admitting humanity's helplessness. **Rectitude** unfurls when every tribe, tongue, people, and nation is named a kingdom of priests—justice sung into being. The scroll is opened, history is interpreted, and worship becomes the engine that drives the mission forward. The apocalypse unveils a civilization of poverty in which the poor become agents of history, precisely like the future God seals in the Lamb.[20]

Notice how the Spirit orchestrates a feast for all the senses: sight (emerald rainbow, jasper throne), sound (harps, incense prayers), touch (elders prostrate), and even taste and smell by implication—the throne-room chant promises a banquet where hunger ends. Jesus models that same culinary discernment when, in his hometown synagogue, he reads Isaiah 61 and declares his anointing of the Spirit "to proclaim good news to the poor" (Luke 4:18–21 ESV). Three lessons follow: First, where politics gropes for meaning, worship proclaims the universe's storyline. Second, diversity is not a decorative backdrop but a necessary harmony—without every language, the song is incomplete. Third, mission flows from doxology; the scroll's judgments descend only after praise ascends, teaching that action detached from adoration soon loses its compass. When worship sets the beat, each saint enters with their voice, and each work keeps pace.

If the earlier *chapulín* tale warned us against power unmoored from virtue, Revelation 5 shows virtue ignited by worship. Here, ambition kneels, tears turn prophetic, and the opened scroll authorizes a people who embody Lamb-shaped power: wounded yet victorious, meek yet sovereign. In practical terms, this means congregations should sing Scripture before they analyze it, name local injustices while the incense is still in the air, and teach new converts to pray in their mother tongue, which is the language the Lamb already hears.

Set beside Mauricio's meadow and Tita's kitchen, the throne-room feast completes our menu: The farm plot, family table, and cosmic banquet form a single trajectory. Each setting tells the same story—creation, fall, redemption—scaled to fit village, nation, and universe. To join the anthem is to eat, work, and worship in ways that echo heaven's chorus: "Amen! Blessing and glory and wisdom and thanksgiving and honor and power and might be to our God forever and ever" (Rev. 7:12 ESV).

A Feast of Balanced Grace

God's mission, I have argued, is neither static creed nor free-floating impulse. It is a living diet whose four staples, **MPSR**, must be tasted in continual rotation. Formation unfolds in a living cycle: Worldview shapes culture, culture shapes lived experience, and fresh experience, reflected upon, refines worldview once more. Doctrine hardens whenever that movement stalls, yet experience drifts when it ignores its roots. The four-flavor matrix—prophetic just, zealous sacred, contemplative vulnerable, and communal noble—maps the diverse "palates" through which congregations journey through the cycle. Taken together, the cycle serves as our compass and the matrix as our menu: The first shows where formation travels; the second supplies the nourishment needed along the road.

Two narratives frame the point: Mauricio the *chapulín* teaches that power untethered from virtue devours the field it seeks to own; Tita's kitchen shows that disciplined passion can feed a wounded household back to hope. Placed side by side, the tales declare that unchecked hunger turns gifts into curses, but sanctified desire turns ordinary resources into sacrament. Revelation 5 widens the lens. Around the Lamb's scroll table, every tribe brings unique seasoning to the feast, proving that the gospel's flavor is deepened, not diluted, when cultures mingle. Liturgical mystagogy safeguards that depth: Baptism, communion, and anointing reset the spiritual chemistry of the church the way breath resets pulse, guiding communities back to stability whenever one staple threatens to crowd out the rest. Latino/a theologians name this alchemy *mestizaje espiritual*—the Spirit blending *lucha*, *fiesta*, and *familia* into a single salsa of grace so that every table tilts toward the poor and every culture's spice deepens the gospel's savor.

Chapter Nine

Cultivating the Spiritual Feast in Christian Communities

Life in the excess of God's love shown as a smile may come to us like rain showers in times of drought, making us laugh.

—Elaine Padilla

What if our faith communities—churches or universities—could offer more than just sermons, lectures, or small gatherings? What if they could host an ongoing spiritual feast where people experience growth and transformation together? Imagine walking into a space where God's presence is acknowledged like salt that enhances every flavor, where people's devotion warms the atmosphere like fat enriching a meal, where moments of quiet reflection cut through confusion like acid sharpening a dish, and where ethical living provides the heat that draws all the elements together. This is the essence of the **MPSR** framework. Think of it as a recipe designed to grow for individuals and entire communities. When we blend these four virtues into our gatherings, we are not just offering spiritual "snacks." We are cooking up real spiritual nourishment that can transform lives and societies contextually.

Just as Latin American magical realism seamlessly weaves the extraordinary into everyday life, spiritual transformation can reshape individuals and entire communities. In *One Hundred Years of Solitude*, Gabriel García Márquez presents levitating priests, raining flowers, and prophetic dreams as natural occurrences, challenging conventional views of reality. Similarly, when godly and ordinary realities intertwine, remarkable change can unfold within a community. Rooted in Indigenous folklore, history, and contemporary struggles, magical realism—seen in the works of Isabel Allende and Jorge Luis Borges—offers a lens for exploring identity, memory, and oppression. Likewise, collective spiritual transformation reveals profound truths, demonstrating how faith and daily life can merge to inspire renewal and lasting impact.

Think about a church where multiple people are undergoing inner renewal. Their energy and excitement can light a spark spreading throughout the

Box 9.1 The MPSR Framework: A Fresh Recipe for Spiritual Growth

Majesty (the Salt)

"Majesty" means recognizing and honoring God's sacred authority. Like salt in cooking, it draws out the richness of other ingredients, helping us see everything in life through a holy and reverent lens. In practical terms, Majesty reminds us to shape our actions with humility and purpose, always mindful of God's greatness.

Piety (the Fat)

"Piety" is about daily devotion, service, and acts of compassion. Picture that satisfying warmth in a well-prepared dish—this is the "fat" that carries flavor and sustains you. When believers consistently practice worship, prayer, and service, the community's faith is enriched and nourished.

Solitude (the Acid)

"Solitude" involves intentional moments of reflection and introspection, which can be as sharp and clarifying as a squeeze of lime or a splash of vinegar in a recipe. It cuts through the noise and helps us refocus on what truly matters, revealing deeper insights into God, ourselves, and our relationships.

Rectitude (the Heat)

"Rectitude" means living ethically and pursuing just relationships. The heat seals flavors together, ensuring everything aligns with God's heart for holiness and justice. Communities anchored in Rectitude model fairness, honesty, and love—not just in words but in tangible actions.

When these four virtues work together, they create an inviting, life-giving environment that enriches personal transformation and communal solidarity. This synergy echoes the spirit of Latin American magical realism, in which everyday life and the miraculous weave together seamlessly.

congregation with cultural hybridity. Mercedes Sosa, famous for her songs of justice and hope, reminds us that this "feast" isn't just for our benefit—it is also for action. Whether discussing the synergy of a local church or a campus ministry, the shared sense of purpose and faith can inspire real change.

Lessons from Jesus, Joseph, and Daniel for Community Transformation

When we reflect on biblical figures like Jesus, Joseph, and Daniel—each living in different times and under various political regimes—it becomes clear how their stories embody the core values of **MPSR**. These leaders show us the importance of creating spiritual gatherings where our communities can honor God's greatness, nurture compassion, reflect deeply, and advocate for justice. For instance, Jesus consistently proclaimed God's sovereignty through his teachings and actions, while Joseph recognized that his talents came from God even while serving in Pharaoh's court. Daniel stood firm in his faith, refusing to worship Babylonian idols and always pointing back to God as the trustworthy source of power and wisdom.

Their lives also demonstrate true devotion. Jesus dedicated himself to daily prayer, healing others, and performing acts of kindness. Joseph stayed faithful and ethical despite his hardships, resisting temptation and trusting God's plan. Daniel maintained a disciplined prayer routine, praying three times daily even when it risked his life. Additionally, they valued moments of reflection—Jesus often withdrew to quiet places to connect with God, Joseph used his time in prison to reflect and prepare, and Daniel's calmness in the lions' den was rooted in his prayerful and thoughtful life.

Finally, these leaders were passionate advocates for justice. Jesus stood up for the marginalized and ultimately sacrificed himself for humanity. Joseph managed Egypt's resources with integrity, saving lives and healing family relationships. Daniel served faithfully in a foreign government, staying true to his beliefs and positively influencing leaders through his righteous actions. These powerful examples inspire churches and universities to create environments where reverence, devotion, reflection, and justice come together. When MPSR is in the community's kitchen, a banquet of spiritual growth and meaningful change is prepared.

Churches and Universities as Spiritual Kitchens

Think of churches and educational institutions as "spiritual kitchens." These are places where people gather to be nourished—in both body and soul—so they can grow and flourish. As Wilmer Estrada-Carrasquillo suggests with his idea of a "trialectical" conversation, these kitchens could bring together identity, context, and public theology.[1] This means they don't just discuss faith in a vacuum; they also consider social, cultural, and personal factors.

Within liberation theology, Ellacuría provides a vivid example of how such "spiritual kitchens" could function.[2] On November 16, 1989, during the Salvadoran Civil War (1980–92), a Salvadoran military unit murdered six Jesuit priests, their housekeeper, and her daughter at the Universidad Centroamericana (UCA) in San Salvador. Among them was Ellacuría, UCA's rector, who had turned the university into a hub of critical inquiry serving the marginalized. The victims were targeted for their advocacy for peace and social justice, and their deaths sparked international condemnation and exposed human rights abuses and foreign involvement in the conflict. Following the model of Jesus, Joseph, and Daniel, Ellacuría insisted that acknowledging God's **Majesty** (the greatness of God's justice) and nurturing ethical commitments must extend beyond pious words to real-world advocacy.

Solidarity in Liberation Theology

Solidarity in liberation theology is a committed, active stance with the oppressed in their fight for justice. More than empathy, it demands praxis—reflection and action—to dismantle systemic inequalities. Theologians like Segundo, Sobrino, and Ellacuría emphasize solidarity as a theological mandate that cultivates social transformation and structural change.

Solidarity, deeply rooted in the life and teachings of Jesus Christ, calls Christians to align with the marginalized, exemplifying Christ's identification with the oppressed. Inspiration from Rutilio Grande shows how this principle can be applied to concrete communities. Grande, a Salvadoran Jesuit priest, devoted himself to the rural poor, walking alongside them and forming small Christian communities that read Scripture considering their struggles. His approach exemplifies how faith becomes action: not charity from afar but mutual participation in one another's burdens. Juan Hernández Pico elaborates in his work that this solidarity is a theological imperative and a transformative response to structural injustice, calling for mutual engagement and shared struggle.[3] From a Pentecostal perspective, Sammy Alfaro's *Divino compañero* focuses on constructing a Hispanic Pentecostal Christology informed by the community's faith, worship, and liberating praxis, which grounds theological frameworks in lived experiences and cultural contexts.[4] Drawing on Ellacuría's emphasis that theology must be grounded in history—"the historicization of faith"—we see that these "spiritual kitchens" cannot stand apart from the realities of injustice. Instead, they must be places where social analysis, moral reflection, and communal worship blend seamlessly, fueling meaningful transformation.

Picture your congregation or campus ministry as a bustling kitchen (a banquet) where people from all walks of life come to be fed—spiritually and sometimes literally. If we consider Wilmer Estrada-Carrasquillo's idea of a trialectical conversation, this spiritual kitchen prioritizes the community's needs. It is not about offering a "one-size-fits-all" meal but about cooking something flavorful and rich that satisfies diverse cultural palates and individual pilgrimages. At the same time, Jon Sobrino—another Jesuit theologian shaped by the Salvadoran context—teaches us to view reality "from the perspective of the crucified peoples."[5] For Sobrino, identifying with the marginalized is not just an extra layer of compassion; it is an essential way of seeing Christ incarnate in the suffering of the poor. In 2007, the Vatican's Congregation for the Doctrine of the Faith (CDF) criticized aspects of Jon Sobrino's Christology, arguing that his focus on Jesus's humanity and solidarity with the poor downplayed his divinity, especially in how he described Jesus's self-awareness and mission. While some saw this as a theological imbalance, many theologians defended Sobrino, saying his work reflected the real struggles of marginalized communities and aligned with liberation theology. The debate highlighted ongoing tensions between traditional doctrine and theology that responds to social injustice. When guided by **MPSR**, communities learn to listen, share power, and respect every individual's dignity, just as Grande and Sobrino insisted the church must stand, without fear, for those most vulnerable in society. Faith isn't something we keep tucked away for Sunday mornings or theology classes; it is woven into real life, empowering us to address real-world needs.

Focusing on **MPSR** creates a holistic faith environment (robust diet) where reverent worship sets the tone, service projects and daily prayer enrich community life, and moments of quiet reflection sharpen each person's sense of purpose. Regularly considering issues of justice and integrity, as advocated by theologians like Pico and Dussel, churches and universities stay attentive to personal transformation and systemic change.[6]

Juan Luis Segundo reminds us that solidarity depends on rigorous social analysis and a willingness to challenge unjust systems.[7] More than emotional empathy or fleeting charity, solidarity requires a thoughtful approach—rooted in theological reflection—that addresses the structural roots of inequality. Segundo's "see-judge-act" methodology equips congregations and campus ministries to engage issues of poverty, racism, and violence in practical and transformative ways. Juan Luis Segundo, a Jesuit theologian and key figure in liberation theology, expanded the see-judge-act method to address systemic injustice through a theological lens. This approach involves observing social realities (see), interpreting them through the gospel and Catholic social teaching (judge), and taking action to create change (act). Segundo saw theology as a dynamic process shaped by the lived experiences of the marginalized, emphasizing that faith must be expressed through solidarity and the pursuit of justice. In this way, faith communities honor God's presence, nurture compassion, cultivate reflection, and act for justice, becoming spaces where spiritual growth and ethical living thrive together.

Embracing Diversity: The "Kale" of Spiritual Life

In spiritual growth—much like a healthy diet—we sometimes need the "kale" that we might not love initially but that does us a world of good. In many Latin American contexts, that "kale" can be found in Indigenous cultures and practices, which intertwine the mystical and the ordinary. Magical realism, for instance, portrays everyday miracles—such as García Márquez's levitating priests or showers of yellow flowers—as usual, offering refreshing ways to experience God's presence in daily life.[8] These practices remind us of the principles of **Rectitude**, recognizing the rights and voices of all people, and **Majesty**, honoring the vastness of God's Creation as understood through diverse cultural lenses. When churches and universities embrace and value these traditions, they are genuinely inclusive and vibrant spiritual environments, staying rooted in the real world while remaining open to wonder and mystery.

Communities embodying the four core elements become spaces where faith is nurtured individually and shared collectively, shaping a more just and spiritually vibrant society. Honoring unique perspectives, they create spaces where the spiritual and material are deeply interconnected, enriching the community's faith experience. Spirituality grows most profound when it honors the voices of many and finds wonder in the ordinary. Table 9.1 outlines practical ways churches and faith communities can cultivate these spiritual dimensions.

Table 9.1 Practical Steps for Implementing MPSR in Communities

Spiritual Element	Practical Application in Churches	Examples from Latine Theology
Majesty	Recognizing God's sovereignty in worship and leadership	Integration of liberation theology with ecclesiology
Piety	Encouraging personal and communal devotion	Grassroots movements like ecclesial base communities
Solitude	Providing spaces for individual reflection	Spiritual retreats influenced by contemplative traditions
Rectitude	Committing to social justice and ethical leadership	Faith-based activism in Latin America

In integrating these elements, faith communities move beyond passive spirituality and engage in an embodied, lived-out faith. Interplaying together tradition, action, personal reflection, and communal solidarity, they become catalysts for transformation—both spiritually and socially.

Hybridity and Inclusivity in Our Shared Spaces

The constant mixing of cultures—through travel, migration, and global communication—reminds us how important it is to build welcoming spiritual spaces. These spiritual kitchens must be big enough for everyone in a globalized era. Drawing inspiration from the communal and justice-driven approach of Grande, we see that every culture, social class, or linguistic group deserves a place at the table.[9] This is where music, art, and storytelling worldwide serve as "seasonings" to enrich our spiritual meals. For instance, Cabral's songs of resistance remind us that worship and art can fuel movements for hope and liberation—realities that theologians like Ellacuría believed were fundamental to the church's mission. Cabral (1937–2011) was an Argentine singer-songwriter, poet, and philosopher known for his music's focus on freedom, social justice, and spiritual reflection in Latin America. His lyrics and storytelling often addressed themes of love, peace, and human dignity, resonating with audiences experiencing political and social struggles. His song "No soy de aquí, ni soy de allá" became widely recognized as an expression of identity beyond borders. A vocal critic of authoritarian regimes and an advocate for personal freedom, Cabral's work influenced cultural and social discourse throughout the region.

The spiritual kitchen must be big enough for everyone in a globalized context marked by migration and cultural blending. Another song from Mercedes Sosa, "Gracias a la Vida," exemplifies how art becomes a vessel for resilience, justice, and hope, resonating deeply with communities seeking transformation.[10] Citing Sosa's biographical pilgrimage, including her advocacy for equality and role in the *Nueva Canción* movement, adds depth to her influence as a symbol of spiritual and social solidarity. The *Nueva Canción* (New Song) movement emerged in Latin America in the mid-twentieth century, blending traditional folk music with socially conscious lyrics. Rooted in struggles for justice and liberation, it became a voice for marginalized communities and a form of resistance against authoritarian regimes. Key artists like Violeta Parra and Víctor Jara in Chile, Mercedes Sosa in Argentina, and Silvio Rodríguez in Cuba shaped the movement, incorporating Indigenous instruments, folkloric styles, and themes of solidarity. Their music addressed poverty, inequality, and human rights abuses while preserving cultural heritage. *Nueva Canción* influenced Latin American music and symbolized resilience and identity during political and social upheaval. Sosa's songs, and many others of resistance and hope, invite communities to commit themselves to the collective struggle for justice, standing in solidarity with individuals from marginalized backgrounds and people facing oppression. When we embrace this cultural blending, our churches and campuses mirror God's Kingdom, where everyone has a seat at the table. Openness to multiculturalism and ongoing change ensures that spiritual communities remain dynamic, inclusive, and truly reflective of the people who call those communities home.

Implementing Change in Church and Campus Life

Churches and universities can begin by hosting gatherings highlighting the richness of multiple cultures. Take these examples where this idea might take shape in a worship service led by Reverend Lucía alongside Professor Alvarez, where traditions as varied as Andean flute music and Southern gospel hymns come together in a single celebration. These events encourage collaboration among individuals from different backgrounds so each person can savor the "spiritual recipes" others bring to the table. In this way, a college student named Marisol, who grew up celebrating Día de Muertos with her family in Mexico, could share this tradition's profound sense of remembrance and community. At the same time, someone else might introduce a more meditative Taizé chant from Europe.[11] Exchanging these flavors of faith, both groups discover new perspectives and fresh inspiration.

Another way to see this is the acts of service, guided by the warmth of **Piety**, then become a vital expression of compassion. Imagine a congregation where Father Delgado, inspired by local needs, starts a small food pantry that soon grows into a tutoring program. Here, the entire community—students, faculty, families—bands together to ensure no child goes without educational support or a hot meal. Through these tangible forms of care, the faith community lives out a devotion that transcends words, much like the comforting fat that gives depth to a hearty meal.

Amid busy schedules and constant demands, creating intentional moments for reflection (**Solitude**) is equally important. Picture a retreat organized by Sister Carmen in a rural setting outside the city, where exhausted students and congregants can retreat from the noise of daily life for a weekend of prayer, journaling, and thoughtful dialogue. Like a splash of acid in a carefully planned dish, these periods help sharpen the community's sense of purpose and keep everyone grounded in the deeper callings of love and justice.

The pursuit of justice, guided by **Rectitude**, weaves itself into the daily decisions of churches and universities. A simple yet powerful example might be when administrators review budgets with transparency, setting aside funds for scholarships that open doors for first-generation Latino students like José or Ana, ensuring they have a real chance at academic success. Similarly, committees might be formed to address ethical concerns, such as fair wage policies for support staff. Each decision becomes an opportunity to align

Box 9.2 Practical Steps for Churches and Universities

- **Host Culturally Rich Gatherings**
  - Plan worship services or campus events that draw on diverse cultural practices. For example, incorporate Salvadoran traditions that honor the legacy of Rutilio Grande, or host lectures on Sobrino's vision of the "crucified peoples." Each cultural or theological ingredient adds depth to the communal feast.
- **Practice Compassion Rooted in Devotion**
  - Commit to local service projects—food pantries, tutoring programs, or community organizing—inspired by Grande's grassroots approach. Let these projects flow from daily prayer and honest reflection on the community's needs, just as Jon Sobrino calls the church to keep the poor at the center of its mission.
- **Schedule Intentional Times for Reflection**
  - Carve out retreats or quiet hours on campus, following Jesus's withdrawal pattern to solitude. Encourage communal reflection on injustice, echoing Segundo's emphasis on analyzing and critiquing the sociopolitical reality before acting.
- **Pursue Justice with Transparency**
  - Align budgets, policies, and initiatives with the ethical mandates of Scripture and liberation theology. Just as Ellacuría emphasized, the gospel must confront systemic oppression and review how funds are allocated to scholarships or staff salaries. Form committees dedicated to ethical standards and equitable treatment, blending **MPSR** with the practical needs of institutions.
- **Honor God's Majesty in Every Gathering**
  - Begin classes, sermons, or staff meetings by acknowledging God's grandeur and the sacredness of human dignity. This daily practice helps keep the community focused on his priorities rather than becoming lost in institutional routines.

Through such tangible actions, faith communities move from mere talk of solidarity to the lived reality of mutual care. Each choice—big or small—becomes an opportunity to express the virtues.

with the heart of God's justice, much like the careful application of heat that melds a dish's flavors into a harmonious whole.

Above all, **Majesty** remains the guiding star in every classroom, sermon, and gathering. When Professor Torres begins each lecture by acknowledging God's grandeur in Creation—or when youth leader Valeria reminds her Sunday school class of the awe-inspiring mystery that weaves through every part of life—this reverence flavors everything the community does. It is as though each ingredient, each cultural tradition, and each act of devotion points back to God's infinite wonder. Through humility and a deep awareness of the other, these efforts to serve and learn become more than programs and events; they become reflections of a love that is at once profound and practical, always honoring the One who gives all life its beauty and purpose.

A Feast That Looks Like the Kingdom of God

When we combine these ideas, we see a spiritual feast—not just a quick meal for personal comfort but a banquet where justice, belonging, and compassion are on the menu. The principles of Latine theology come to life when individual growth blends with communal sharing, embodying Christ's love in everything we do.

When **MPSRs** find their way into everything a community does—whether in a church youth group led by Sister Carmen or a university lecture taught by Professor Torres—something remarkable happens: The entire congregation or campus becomes a living "banquet" of spiritual formation. This echoes Paulo Freire's understanding that authentic learning and transformation involve ongoing cycles of reflection and action, refined by the collective spirit. Juan Hernández Pico's emphasis on solidarity adds another layer, reminding us that prayer and worship should overflow into tangible efforts for justice and liberation.[12] Meanwhile, the powerful voice of Mercedes Sosa provides a steady soundtrack to this pilgrimage, her songs weaving stories of hope and resistance that lift marginalized voices. In such a setting, art and faith merge seamlessly, stirring hearts to see God's **Majesty** in everyday life and emboldening people to act on behalf of those who need it most.

Practical Takeaways

I have claimed that Rolheiser's *The Holy Longing* offers a balanced framework for Christian spirituality but does not fully address the modern faith's sociopolitical and cultural complexities.[13] In contrast, the **MPSR** framework provides a more dynamic and justice-oriented approach. When churches and universities blend reverence, devotion, sustained reflection, and ethical action, they can confront systemic injustice and foster genuine transformation. Whereas Rolheiser stresses mellowness and community, **MPSR** adds the fire of righteous anger and the richness of cultural engagement, offering a practical model for change that reshapes both personal lives and society.

As we come to the close of our exploration, picture the church or university as a bustling kitchen, alive with conversation, music, and the aromas of a meal prepared in faith. We bring the **MPSR** recipe into this space, each virtue providing an essential flavor in the shared feast of spiritual growth. When we begin by centering ourselves on God's awe-inspiring presence, commit to acts of devotion and service, create intentional times of reflection, and ground every choice in what is right, we serve up a banquet that nourishes not only individual hearts but the greater community and world beyond.

Heed the legacy of Ellacuría, Segundo, Sobrino, Grande, and many more who were assassinated: Where every ingredient is seasoned with God's abundant love, faith communities become a banquet of justice, solidarity, and communion.[14] Within this vision of a spiritual kitchen, a few guiding principles can help us realize it. The first is *a resounding celebration of cultural richness*, drawing on local traditions—like those Grande supported in rural El Salvador—and global Christian influences. The second is prioritizing people over efficiency, continually asking whether a new program truly upholds the dignity of those most in need. Another key is to stay adaptive, taking regular stock of what works and what doesn't, just as Segundo's methodology insists on critical reflection and flexible action. We also do well in *leveraging the arts*, weaving music and storytelling into our worship and teaching, much like Mercedes Sosa's songs of hope. Finally, include diverse voices, reflecting Estrada-Carrasquillo's trialectical approach—so that no one is left out of the conversation.

Ultimately, this shared table is about more than just meeting personal needs; it is about participating in God's ongoing work of justice, solidarity, and compassion. Whoever you are—pastor, student, professor, or volunteer—there is a seat for you here, where every dish is seasoned by love, every voice matters, and every heart is invited to grow. Elaine Padilla reminds us that "life in the excess of God's love shown as a smile may come to us like rain showers in times of drought, making us laugh." This vision captures the heart of what **MPSR** offers—a framework for experiencing God's love fully, transforming drought-stricken lives and communities into flourishing gardens of hope and joy.

So roll up your sleeves, gather around, and build it together. As we prepare, serve, and share this holy meal, we catch glimpses of God's Kingdom among us—a place where majesty meets everyday life, devotion mingles with action, reflection sharpens purpose, and righteousness sizzles with prophetic energy.

Chapter Ten

The Watermelonless Tree

You cannot reap what you do not sow.

No puedes cosechar lo que no siembras.
Have you ever seen a watermelon grow in a tree?
We all know, watermelons do not grow on trees.
They grow from vines, spreading across
the ground in open spaces.
But today, many look for watermelons
growing in trees, discovering ways
to harm others in His name. In contrast,
the true message of Jesus is a *peacemaking*
message that spreads across the ground in open spaces.
The word that bothers many is liberation—saving individuals,
Christ's deliverance, calling the world
to love one another right now in the present.
Nadie me detendrá; El Espíritu del Señor está sobre mí.
You cannot reap what you do not sow.
Liberation means redemption, freeing people
from the many types of slavery.
Liberation means there is no exploitation of man
by man in the world, nor Creation exploitation by men.
Slavery is illiteracy. Slavery is hunger or the inability
to buy food. Slavery is the lack of a roof,
not having a place to live. Slavery is misery.
The Love of the Lord surrounds all people,

this loving-kindness grows from his essence
of being a Creator of Love. *What else do we expect?*

I am the Brown Church.
God calls me mija/mijo.

This message of Jesus, a peacemaking message
that spreads across the ground in open spaces.
You cannot reap what you do not sow.
No puedes cosechar lo que no siembras.

This graceful love, incarnated in Christ, who led
us to liberation like those who were freed from slavery
in Egypt—his people were cared for while they were driven to exile.
This liberating Jesus, the source of our essence,
the essence of God. When we embody the Holy Spirit,
we liberate kindness, filling the land with joy.
Remember Joseph in Egypt, remember Daniel in Babylon—
the Presence of God's people is not about the nation in power.
It's for God's glory among the nations. Like many,
our country struggles with globalization,
promoting division, rage, and hate.
How are we to respond to this new globalization?
We have the opportunity as Spirit-filled Christians
to walk this earth, not for the values and principles
that cultivate this hate. We are obligated to act
in the emptiness that joins in the suffering and sacrifice
of Christ. We aim to find peace in the Spirit of Peace
to free ourselves from slavery. By suffering and rising
from the cross, we liberate ourselves and transport
the Kingdom of God throughout this nation as exiles.

Yo siento a Dios de otro modo.

This message of Jesus, a peacemaking message
spreading across the ground in open spaces.

You cannot reap what you do not sow.
No puedes cosechar lo que no siembras.

To be in Christ is to see the history
in which we live as God's progressive revelation
in every human face. *"He who sees Me sees the Father."*
This is true for every human being, according
to Matthew 25, the action in front of a person
is an action in front of God:
If you give food or drink, you give to Me.
If you deny it, you deny it to Me.
It is not how a person speaks of God
that lets us know if the fire of Love has passed,
but how they talk of human things.

Recobrando la misión integral del Señor.

You cannot reap what you do not sow.
No puedes cosechar lo que no siembras.

It is time to break comfort and fear
to spread across the ground in open spaces.
It is a time to dare to dream the audacity
of the improbable, of the impossible.
And opt for intervention which is possible.
Action is an art where the quality of our
personal and political relationship
with specific people and the social fabric
in which we live is measured.

You cannot reap what you do not sow.
No puedes cosechar lo que no siembras.

You cannot reap what you do not sow.

Conclusion

Sowing Transformation Seeds

Theological knowledge should not function as a mechanism that generates dehumanizing discourses or legitimizes systems of domination, but rather as a principle of liberation.

—María Pilar Aquino

As we conclude this exploration of sainthood, we recognize that true theological wisdom is a "robust spiritual diet," nourishing the soul like a harmonious diet sustains the body. The four core elements—**MPSR**—offer the foundation for personal growth and communal transformation, urging us beyond doctrines that perpetuate oppression or justify systems of domination. Instead, theological insight should liberate, inspiring active solidarity. This wisdom must be planted to witness the fruits of liberation. My poem, *The Watermelonless Tree*, reflects this vision, sowing seeds for a just and compassionate society, calling saints to transform faith into active love. I invite saints to embrace solidarity, walk humbly alongside the marginalized, and cultivate dignity, justice, and grace communities.

Latine theology has profoundly shaped American society, influencing its culture, economy, and civic life. Through activism, the arts, entrepreneurship, and faith, they infuse resilience, creativity, and a deep commitment to community. Their contributions remain a living force, guiding the nation's moral and social conscience. With this hybridity, *mestizaje*—central to Latine identity—embodies a cultural reality and a metaphor for Latinos' impact on the United States. Through diverse perspectives, labor, and leadership in education, business, and social movements, Latine's theory enriches a more inclusive, dynamic society. Their ongoing contributions reflect a theology of belonging that transcends borders and bridges cultures. Rooted in faith, they tirelessly champion social equity, advocating for immigrants, workers, and marginalized groups. Their civil rights, economic, and political contributions embody a biblical call to justice and hospitality, shaping a society where faith is personal devotion and public commitment in solidarity.

When I arrived in the United States in middle school, a slight cultural difference struck me: how people approached a simple bag of chips. In my home country, Mexico, sharing snacks was second nature—a gesture that said, "You are my friend; we are in this together," even if it was just a handful of chips. But here, when I instinctively offered my chips to those around me, I was met with polite surprise or gentle refusals, as if to say, "Those are yours; sharing isn't expected." In the United States, fairness seemed tied more to individual ownership—if you bought it, it was yours alone to enjoy. This experience of my *cuento* (or my magical realism) highlighted how justice and fairness can take on different meanings based on cultural roots. For me, sharing reflected a sense of justice, a way to connect and show care for others. Through this lens, I began to see how spiritual wholeness, like justice, transcends tradition; it invites us to weave our unique threads into the communal fabric of faith. As we blend these practices into everyday life, we transform faith into a vibrant pilgrimage. Every saint writes their *cuento* with the diet they choose in their reality.

Diets—we all have them. It is about consciously recognizing the nutrients we lack to create the most fulfilling, resource-rich experience within the wholeness of God. To truly understand God, one must commit to justice—a foundational aspect of **MPSR**'s liberation-focused spiritual diet that extends beyond individual entitlement. This spiritual nourishment teaches that knowledge of the spirituality of saints is inseparable from actions that uplift and defend those in hardship. Here, spiritual formation evolves into active justice, embodying God's alignment with the suffering as we take our places as queens or kings, priests, mystics, and warriors. The reality each of us lives in is unique, so the nutrients we need are not the same for everyone. Yet ideologies often try to provide a cohesive understanding of which values should guide all lives. In **MPSR**, justice is not an addition to spirituality but its essence, refusing to justify systems of inequality and instead challenging them.

Our realities are unique, so the nutrients we need are not the same for everyone; however, ideologies commonly suggest a normative vision of what those "nutrients" should be for a healthy society. Just as salt, fat, acid, and heat are essential to culinary mastery, a spiritually nourishing life critiques oppressive social, economic, and political structures, calling believers to dismantle these forces in the name of human dignity and Christ's teachings. Justice in this vision moves beyond ritual and private practice, extending into public advocacy and collective action. This liberation-focused path redefines justice as central to faith, inspiring transformative social engagement that connects spirituality with the lived realities of marginalized societies. As Latine theology teaches, faith is enriched through cultural hybridity, creating a vibrant spiritual diet that welcomes all and weaving diverse traditions into our expressions of faith.

Each life needs proper nourishment, yet the world often serves a single dish. In Latine theology, the finest theologians are chefs who blend imagination and awareness into the rich stew of their lived reality. In the spirit of Mercedes Sosa's "Gracias a la Vida," we are reminded that embracing the beauty of life involves recognizing the struggles and resilience of all communities, particularly those historically marginalized. This song echoes the call for justice and solidarity, reinforcing that our spiritual diet is enriched by the diverse voices and experiences shaping our collective pilgrimage. Honoring these narratives, we cultivate a more compassionate and inclusive society where everyone is valued and celebrated, ultimately nourishing our shared humanity.

Central to this spiritual diet are foundational pillars that begin with a theological understanding rooted in sacred and cultural humility. Just as sharing a simple bag of chips in Mexico reflected community and solidarity, so too is the call for saints to observe and respect diverse cultural practices without judgment, guided by heavenly wisdom (2 Pet. 1:3). This approach acknowledges culture as dynamic and urges the faithful to align actions with God's will with empathy rather than imposing rigid judgments. A spiritual diet becomes a pilgrimage of observing and learning, positioning believers as humble stewards of justice rather than agents of domination. Recognizing and respecting these cultural differences can bridge divides, encouraging empathy and understanding across cultural lines.

Practical applications of this spiritual diet call for embodying Christ's compassion, bridging cultural divides, and ensuring that the Christian message remains accessible and meaningful across diverse settings. Saints are encouraged to actively reflect Christ's compassion by adapting their approach to connect genuinely with different cultures, making faith a shared, inclusive experience that honors the values and experiences of others. Recognizing and adapting to cultural dynamics highlights the importance of understanding cultural influences on worldviews and staying attentive to shifts within these perspectives. Equipped with godly wisdom, saints must remain relevant and reflect God's love through sincere, respectful relationships. Rather than viewing culture as an obstacle, this approach positions it as a valuable tool for understanding and love, challenging believers to engage constructively with the world's diversity.

Empathetic engagement is essential within this spiritual diet, urging saints to embrace and honor cultural values, transforming communication into a bridge for sharing the teachings of Jesus in ways that deeply resonate. Saints uphold meaningful transformation and understanding by respecting these values, moving beyond superficial evangelization toward profound cultural engagement. A core insight in the spiritual diet of **MPSR** reframes poverty as a condition born not of inevitability but of human choices and social structures. This view challenges believers to recognize poverty because of systemic injustice, calling individuals and societies responsible for many deprivations and indignities. Theologically, this spiritual diet envisions justice as life-giving while viewing poverty as an assault on life itself, urging action for those from marginalized backgrounds.

Justice within this spiritual diet is seen through a communal lens, where sharing resources—even as simple as a bag of chips—reinforces solidarity and mutual care, emphasizing collective well-being and genuine bonds. This call redefines spirituality, urging believers beyond acts of charity toward a deep identification with the struggles of marginalized individuals. It promotes compassionate, empathetic engagement, positioning believers as active participants in the realities of those facing injustice. Solidarity thus becomes a bridge from contemplation to action, where faith meets praxis. This shift transforms the spiritual diet into one rooted in active, transformative love, aligning the faithful with the lives and experiences of the oppressed. Small acts of sharing become meaningful practices of fairness and compassion, underscoring the importance of mutual care within a community.

Table C.1 Cultural Engagement Framework for Christian Spirituality

Category	Elements	Description
Theological Foundations	Sacred power and cultural understanding, knowledge of God, and observation without judgment	Saints understand culture as a dynamic entity and observe it without judgment, aligning their actions with wisdom and God's authority (2 Pet. 1:3).
Practical Applications	Christ's compassion and cultural compassion, alignment with Christian message	Saints embody Christ's compassion, adapting their communication to bridge cultural gaps and align with Christian teachings, making the faith accessible and resonant in diverse settings.
Cultural Dynamics and Adaptation	Recognition of cultural influence, preparedness for the future, and godly wisdom	Saints recognize the influence of culture on worldviews and stay abreast of cultural shifts to remain relevant and prepared, using culture as a tool to reflect God's love and connect with diverse communities.
Empathetic Engagement	Owning cultural values, transformative communication	Saints identify unique cultural values and communicate the teachings of Jesus in ways that resonate with the transformation of those values and deeper understanding across cultures.

This spiritual diet uses concepts of fairness and justice. **MPSR** presents God as an advocate for the oppressed, embodying the preferential option for the poor. Here, God is not a distant figure but a compassionate ally to those denied justice, calling believers to align their actions with the needs of marginalized communities. This perspective resonates with the God of the exodus, who liberated the Israelites, and Christ, who identified with the "least of these." It challenges believers to embody Christlike solidarity, moving from passive belief to active alignment with justice, compassion, and liberation.

Adopting this spiritual diet may require rethinking concepts of fairness and justice, a challenge exemplified by Judy Baca's work in Los Angeles. For example, Baca's *The Great Wall of Los Angeles* is a mural highlighting California's history from the perspective of marginalized communities, emphasizing social justice, historical reclamation, and community empowerment. Her advocacy for marginalized communities reflects **MPSR**'s vision of God as an ally for the oppressed, embodying the preferential option for the poor. Vaca demonstrates that God is not distant but intimately engaged with those in need, urging believers to align their actions with the struggles of the overlooked. Her efforts resonate with the God of the exodus and Christ's identification with the "least of these" (Matt. 25:45), challenging us to transform passive belief into active engagement, embodying solidarity, compassion, and liberation.

In its commitment to empathetic engagement and cultural adaptation, this spiritual "diet" encourages learning from people experiencing lack, whose resilience and solidarity reveal the beauty of communal life and human attachment. Their openness to share, support, and uplift one another exemplifies a form of justice rooted in community care, where small acts of kindness strengthen bonds and a spirit of shared humanity. This willingness to extend even the little one possesses reflects a profound sense of inclusivity and mutual respect, embodying a justice that is both compassionate and communal.

From these experiences, saints are invited to envision a world where justice is inseparably woven with compassion, transcending individualism to become a collective commitment to care for one another. In this light, justice transforms from an individual right to a shared responsibility that builds collective strength and solidarity. The spiritual diet of **MPSR** offers a transformative vision of faith, challenging each person to embody justice not as a distant or rigid concept but as a series of small, intentional acts that honor human dignity and cultivate love. Our spirituality must channel righteous anger into organized, purposeful action, becoming a force for change.

My friend and mentor Elizabeth Conde-Frazier has described spirituality as a relationship with God made real in Christ, which requires discernment and responsiveness to the Spirit's guidance. She is a theologian, educator, and advocate for contextualized Christian education, emphasizing faith and social justice in multicultural communities. As a cofounder of the Association for Hispanic Theological Education (AETH), she promotes accessible theological training for Latinx communities. Her scholarship, including *A Many Colored Kingdom: Multicultural Dynamics for Spiritual Formation*, highlights diversity, community engagement, and practical theology. Her work equips leaders to address systemic inequities through mission practices rooted in relational and incarnational ministry.

The Spirit reveals new truths, urging us to revisit and challenge our theology to meet the needs of our time. As Paul teaches, only those led by the Spirit can discern God's will, for the Spirit transcends and transforms conventional understanding (1 Cor. 2:14–15). This dynamic relationship with the Spirit calls us to remain attuned to God's voice in the present, allowing our spirituality to evolve with new insights while remaining rooted in foundational beliefs. In doing so, we permit the Spirit to roll back the stones of oppression and despair, bringing liberation to the oppressed and the oppressors. Such transformative spirituality—blending priestly contemplation with prophetic action—embodies justice, love, and courage at the heart of our faith.

Incorporating Latine voices and perspectives is vital to nurturing a spiritual diet that embodies inclusivity and justice in our *cuentos*. Amplifying these voices, we recognize the rich cultural contributions of Latine communities, allowing their stories and wisdom to nourish our collective understanding. Engaging the community through open dialogues and cultural celebrations in an environment where diverse experiences are valued and embraced enriches our spiritual pilgrimage within these realities. Inclusive education is a foundation for connecting with the broader spectrum of human experiences, enhancing our empathy and compassion. Mentorship programs and storytelling platforms empower Latine youth, ensuring their voices resonate in shaping our shared future. Advocating for equity within this spiritual framework reinforces the idea that justice is a communal responsibility, reminding us that our spiritual health depends on the well-being of all. These practices cultivate a compassionate and just relational society where everyone is seen, heard, and valued, enriching our spiritual diet.

In resonance with my poem, *The Watermelonless Tree*, the spiritual diet of **MPSR** invites saints to embrace a transformative vision of justice grounded in liberation, compassion, and interdependence. This call aligns with the essence of Almafuerte's poetry, which emphasizes the importance of planting seeds of love and peace. His poetry exemplifies the use of literature for social justice, particularly in works like *¡Avanti!* and *¡Piú Avanti!* His writings encourage resilience and perseverance in adversity, echoing liberation theology's emphasis on human dignity and the fight against oppression. By critiquing societal inequalities and inspiring action, Almafuerte's poetry is a powerful example of how art can challenge injustice and promote transformative change. His famous phrase "*El que no sabe es como el que no ve*" reminds us that awareness and understanding are crucial in our pilgrimage toward justice. Almafuerte's work urges us to remain open to everyday moments that seek freedom from exploitation and uphold human dignity, much as Cabral and others did with his art. Rather than a path to passive spirituality, this diet encourages us to embody the "audacity of the improbable," challenging us to actively dismantle inequality and bring God's Kingdom closer as we transform.

Everyone needs something different to thrive in healthy spiritual forms, but the world often gives us all the same thing. When love and justice guide our actions, hope flourishes. Every kind act is like planting a seed for a better, more complete world. The aim of my book, *Art of Sainthood*, lies not in finding the perfect diet but in cultivating a way of living that adapts to the present reality, where every encounter with goodness in others stretches us toward greater unity—for the sake of God. With my poem's imagery as a guiding vision, this spirituality spreads like "a peacemaking message across open spaces," calling each of us to embody Christ's liberating kindness, recognize God's presence in every face, and affirm our shared pilgrimage. It challenges us to live in solidarity with the poor and the oppressed, cultivating a society that reflects Christlike love and justice—a hopeful, inclusive pilgrimage that sows seeds for a transformative harvest. This shared spiritual formation reminds us, saints, that we truly "cannot reap what we do not sow."

Justice sown in love yields a harvest of hope; in every revolutionary act of MPSR, we plant the seeds of a world made whole.

Notes

Foreword

1 Dallas Willard, *The Great Omission: Reclaiming Jesus's Essential Teachings on Discipleship* (HarperOne, 2006), 62.

2 From Thomas Merton, *New Seeds of Contemplation* (New Directions, 2007), 31.

3 Léon Bloy, *The Woman Who Was Poor* (St. Augustine's Press, 2022).

Introduction

1 Samin Nosrat, *Salt, Fat, Acid, Heat: Mastering the Elements of Good Cooking* (Simon & Schuster, 2017).

2 Some of these works include: (1) Samuel Escobar, *Diálogo entre Cristo y Marx* (Editorial Caribe, 1970); (2) Samuel Escobar, C. René Padilla, Edwin M. Yamauchi, *¿Quién es Cristo Hoy?* (Ediciones Certeza, 1970); and (3) Pedro Arana, Samuel Escobar, and René Padilla, *Progreso, Técnica y Hombre* (Ediciones Puma, 1982).

3 Anette Christensen, *Mercedes Sosa—the Voice of Hope: My Life-Transforming Encounter* (Denmark: Bureau of Business Development, 2019); Ernesto Cardenal, *Gospel in Solentiname* (Wipf & Stock, 2020); Facundo Cabral, *Ayer soñé que podía y hoy puedo* (Librería y Editorial Alsina, 2011); Karen Kerschen, *Violeta Parra: By the Whim of the Wind* (ABQ Press, 2010).

4 Robert Chao Romero, *Brown Church: Five Centuries of Latina/o Social Justice, Theology, and Identity* (InterVarsity Press, 2020).

5 Juan Miguel Zunzunegui, *Hernán Cortés: Encuentro y Conquista* (Grijalbo, 2020).

6 Carmen Nanko-Fernández, *Theologizing en Espanglish* (Orbis, 2014).

7 Ronald Rolheiser, *The Holy Longing: The Search for a Christian Spirituality* (Doubleday, 2014).

8 Richard J. Foster, *Streams of Living Water: Essential Practices from the Six Great Traditions of Christian Faith* (HarperCollins, 2001).

9 Nanko-Fernández, *Theologizing en Espanglish.*

10 C. René Padilla, *What Is Integral Mission?* (Fortress Publishers, 2021).

11 Gustavo Gutiérrez, *We Drink from Our Own Wells: The Spiritual Journey of a People* (Orbis, 2003).

12 Leonardo Boff, *Cry of the Earth, Cry of the Poor* (Orbis, 1997), 42–45; Pablo Richard, *Death of Christendom, Birth of the Church: Historical Analysis and Theological Interpretations* (Orbis, 1987), 128–30; Enrique Dussel, *Ethics of Liberation: In the Age of Globalization and Exclusion* (Duke University Press, 2013), 89–90.

13 José Míguez Bonino, *Doing Theology in a Revolutionary Situation* (Fortress, 1975), 86.

14 Elsa Támez, *Bible of the Oppressed* (Orbis Books, 1982), 102–5; Ivone Gebara, *Longing for Running Water: Ecofeminism and Liberation* (Fortress, 1999), 88–90.
15 Orlando E. Costas, *Liberating News: A Theology of Contextual Evangelization* (Wipf & Stock, 2002).
16 Ignacio Ellacuría, *Freedom Made Flesh: The Mission of Christ and His Church* (Orbis, 1976), 120; Juan Luis Segundo, *The Liberation of Theology* (Orbis, 1976), 55–57; Jon Sobrino, *The True Church and the Poor* (Orbis, 1984), 22–23.
17 Marcella Althaus-Reid, *Indecent Theology: Theological Perversions in Sex, Gender, and Politics* (Routledge, 2000), 15–18.
18 Jose David Rodriguez and Loida I. Martell-Otero, eds., *Teología en conjunto: A Collaborative Hispanic Protestant Theology* (Westminster John Knox, 1997).
19 John Donne, *Devotions upon Emergent Occasions, Together with Death's Duel*, ed. Anthony Raspa (McGill-Queen's University Press, 1975).
20 Thomas Merton, *No Man Is an Island* (Harcourt, Brace, Jovanovic, 1955).
21 José Míguez Bonino, *For Life and Against Death: A Theology That Takes Sides* (Abingdon Press, 1979).
22 José Míguez Bonino, "For Life and Against Death: A Theology That Takes Sides," *Religion Online*, accessed April 16, 2025, https://www.religion-online.org/article/for-life-and-against-death-a-theology-that-takes-sides/.
23 US Department of Health and Human Services, Office of Minority Health (2023), "Hispanic/Latino Health," https://minorityhealth.hhs.gov/hispaniclatino-health.
24 United Nations Economic Commission for Latin America and the Caribbean (ECLAC) (2022), "The World Has 8 Billion People, 662 Million of Whom Live in Latin America and the Caribbean," November 14, 2022, https://www.cepal.org/en/news/world-has-8-billion-people-662-million-whom-live-latin-america-and-caribbean.
25 Héctor Varela-Rios, "Sancochando una antropología Teológica: Un 'sopón' puertorriqueño como método heurístico," *Perspectivas* 15 (2018): 23.
26 G. Arellano, *Taco USA: How Mexican Food Conquered America* (Scribner, 2013).
27 Pope Paul VI, *Evangelii nuntiandi* [Apostolic Exhortation on Evangelization in the Modern World] (Libreria Editrice Vaticana, 1975).
28 Virgilio Elizondo, *Galilean Journey: The Mexican-American Promise* (Orbis, 2000).
29 Óscar Garcia-Johnson, *The Mestizo/a Community of the Spirit: A Postmodern Latino/a Ecclesiology* (Wipf & Stock, 2009).
30 Saint Augustine, *The City of God*, trans. Henry Bettenson (Penguin, 2003).

Chapter One—How a Robust Spiritual Diet Can Feed the Soul

1 Ada María Isasi-Diaz and Fernando F. Segovia, eds., *Hispanic/Latino Theology: Challenge and Promise* (Fortress, 1996).
2 Pope Paul VI, "Address to the Members of the Consilium de Laicis," *Acta Apostolicae Sedis* 66 (Oct. 2, 1974): 568.
3 Second Vatican Council, "Lumen Gentium: Dogmatic Constitution on the Church," in *Vatican Council II: The Conciliar and Post Conciliar Documents*, ed. Austin Flannery (Costello, 1975), 350–426.
4 Virgilio P. Elizondo, *Guadalupe: Mother of the New Creation* (Orbis, 1997).

5 Roberto Goizueta, *Caminemos con Jesús: Toward a Hispanic/Latino Theology of Accompaniment* (Orbis, 1995).

6 Jeanette Rodríguez, *Our Lady of Guadalupe: Faith and Empowerment among Mexican-American Women* (University of Texas Press, 1994).

7 Horacio Bojorge, *Teologías deicidas: El pensamiento de Juan Luis Segundo en su contexto* (Editorial Vórtice, 2008).

8 Ana María, Pineda, *Rutilio Grande: Memory and Legacy of a Jesuit Martyr* (Lectio Publishing, 2022).

9 Elizondo, *Galilean Journey.*

10 "Utopia and Prophecy in Latin America: An Historical Perspective," in *Toward a Society That Serves Its People: The Intellectual Contribution of El Salvador's Murdered Jesuits*, ed. John Hassett and Hugh Lacey (Georgetown University Press, 1991), 125–48.

11 Michael Edward Lee, *Ignacio Ellacuría: Essays on History, Liberation, and Salvation* (Orbis Books, 2013).

12 See Second Vatican Council, "Lumen Gentium: Dogmatic Constitution on the Church," 350–426.

13 E. P. Sanders, *Judaism: Practice and Belief, 63 BCE–66 CE* (SCM, 1992).

14 Jacob Neusner, *The Pharisees: Rabbinic Perspectives* (Hendrickson, 2003).

15 Geza Vermes, *The Complete Dead Sea Scrolls in English* (Penguin Classics, 2004).

16 Flavius Josephus, *The Jewish War*, trans. G. A. Williamson (Penguin, 1970).

17 Marcus J. Borg and John Dominic Crossan, *The Last Week: What the Gospels Really Teach about Jesus's Final Days in Jerusalem* (HarperOne, 2006).

18 Marcus J. Borg, *The Heart of Christianity: Rediscovering a Life of Faith* (HarperCollins, 2004).

19 Justo L. González, *The Mestizo Augustine: A Theologian between Two Cultures* (InterVarsity Press, 2016).

20 Rafael F. Narváez, *Afro-Latin American Theology: Religion, Race, and Justice* (Orbis, 2020).

21 Elsa Támez, *The Many Faces of God: Liberation Theologies from the Developing World* (Orbis, 2006).

Chapter Two—Eat Your Kale and Also Your Avocado

1 Ignacio Ellacuría, *Freedom Made Flesh: The Mission of Christ and His Church*, trans. John Drury (Orbis Books, 1976).

2 Pedro Pablo Sacristán, "Gorg, el gigante," *Cuentos para dormir*, ECURed, accessed April 16, 2025, https://www.ecured.cu/Gorg,_el_gigante_(cuento).

3 Ada María Isasi-Díaz, *En la lucha / In the Struggle: Elaborating a Mujerista Theology* (Fortress, 2004).

4 Lesslie Newbigin, *The Gospel in a Pluralist Society* (Eerdmans, 1989).

5 Gustavo Gutiérrez, *A Theology of Liberation: History, Politics, and Salvation* (Orbis, 1988).

6 Gutiérrez, *We Drink from Our Own Wells.*

7 Pilcher explores how Mexican culinary traditions have evolved through cultural exchange and innovation. See Jeffrey M. Pilcher, *Planet Taco: A Global History of Mexican Food* (Oxford University Press, 2012).
8 Elizabeth Carmichael and Chloë Sayer, *The Skeleton at the Feast: The Day of the Dead in Mexico* (University of Texas, 1991).
9 Enrique Dussel, *Ethics and the Theology of Liberation* (Orbis, 2013).
10 Darrell L. Guder and Lois Barrett, *Missional Church: A Vision for the Sending of the Church in North America* (Eerdmans, 1998).
11 Óscar García-Johnson, *Spirit Outside the Gate: Decolonial Pneumatologies of the American Global South* (InterVarsity Press, 2019).
12 José Comblin, *Theology of Mission* (Orbis, 1997).
13 Mark R. Peacock, "Translating the Biblical Hebrew Word *Nephesh* in Light of New Research," *The Expository Times* 130, no. 1 (2019): 12–19.
14 Daniel C. Fredericks, "Nepheš," in *New International Dictionary of Old Testament Theology and Exegesis*, vol. 3, ed. Willem A. VanGemeren (Zondervan, 1997), 133–34.
15 R. Laird Harris, Gleason L. Archer Jr., and Bruce K. Waltke, eds., *Theological Wordbook of the Old Testament* (Moody Press, 1980).
16 Gutiérrez, *Theology of Liberation.*
17 Gutiérrez, *We Drink from Our Own Wells.*
18 David J. Bosch, *Transforming Mission: Paradigm Shifts in Theology of Mission* (Orbis, 2011).
19 David Cranston, *Mission as Transformation: Learning from Catalysts* (Wipf & Stock, 2014).
20 Leonardo Boff, *Holy Trinity, Perfect Community* (Orbis, 2000).
21 Orlando E. Costas, *Christ Outside the Gate: Mission beyond Christendom* (Wipf & Stock, 2005).
22 Andrew Finlay Walls, *The Missionary Movement in Christian History: Studies in the Transmission of Faith* (Orbis, 1996).
23 Robert J. Alexander, *Prophets of the Revolution: Profiles of Latin American Leaders* (Creative Media Partners, 2018).
24 Humberto Belli, *Beyond Liberation Theology* (Baker, 1993).
25 John Gregory Dunne, *Delano: The Story of the California Grape Strike* (University of California, 2008); Isacio Pérez Fernández, *Fray Bartolomé de las Casas, O.P.: De Defensor de los Indios a Defensor de los Negros* (Editorial San Esteban, 1995); Óscar García-Johnson, *Spirit Outside the Gate: Decolonial Pneumatologies of the American Global South* (InterVarsity Press, 2019).
26 Ada María Isasi-Díaz, *Mujerista Theology: A Theology for the Twenty-First Century* (Orbis, 1996).
27 Phillip Berryman, *Liberation Theology: Essential Facts about the Revolutionary Movement in Latin America and Beyond* (Temple University Press, 1987).
28 Elsa Támez, *The Amnesty of Grace: Justification by Faith from a Latin American Perspective* (Abingdon, 1993).
29 Leonardo Boff, *Cry of the Earth, Cry of the Poor* (Orbis, 1997).
30 Jon Sobrino, *Jesus the Liberator: A Historical-Theological Reading of Jesus of Nazareth* (Orbis, 1993).

31 Paulo Freire, *Pedagogy of the Oppressed* (Bloomsbury, 1970).
32 Ignacio Martín-Baró, *Writings for a Liberation Psychology* (Harvard University Press, 1994).
33 Margaret Randall, *Sandino's Daughters Revisited: Feminism in Nicaragua* (Rutgers University, 1994); Diana Taylor, *Disappearing Acts: Spectacles of Gender and Nationalism in Argentina's Dirty War* (Duke University Press, 1997); Óscar Romero, *The Violence of Love* (Harper & Row, 1985).
34 Christian Smith, *The Emergence of Liberation Theology: Radical Religion and Social Movement Theory* (University of Chicago, 1991).
35 Nanko-Fernández, *Theologizing en Espanglish.*

Chapter Three—Exploring the Spiritual Building Blocks

1 Urban T. Holmes III, *A History of Christian Spirituality: An Analytical Introduction* (Seabury Press, 1981).
2 C. René Padilla, *Mission between the Times: Essays on the Kingdom* (Eerdmans, 1985); Samuel Escobar, *The New Global Mission: The Gospel from Everywhere to Everyone* (InterVarsity Press, 2003).
3 Jon Sobrino, *Christology at the Crossroads: A Latin American Approach* (Orbis, 1978).
4 Romero, *Violence of Love.*
5 Boff, *Cry of the Earth, Cry of the Poor.*
6 Padilla, *Mission between the Times.*
7 Escobar, *New Global Mission.*
8 Ivone Gebarra, *Longing for Running Water: Ecofeminism and Liberation* (Fortress Press, 1999).
9 Matt Eisenbrandt, *Assassination of a Saint: The Plot to Murder Óscar Romero and the Quest to Bring His Killers to Justice* (University of California Press, 2017).
10 Juan F. Sepúlveda, *Pentecostalism and Liberation Theology: A Symbiotic Relationship* (Wipf & Stock, 2013).
11 Boff, *Cry of the Earth, Cry of the Poor.*
12 Elizabeth Conde-Frazier and S. Steve Kang, *A Many Colored Kingdom: Multicultural Dynamics for Spiritual Formation* (Baker, 2004).
13 Sepúlveda, *Pentecostalism and Liberation Theology.*
14 John of the Cross, *Dark Night of the Soul* (Penguin, 2003).
15 René Terranova, *Manual de Guerra Espiritual* (Casa Creación, 2006).
16 Elizondo, *Galilean Journey.*
17 Nancy Pineda-Madrid, *The Holy Spirit: Setting the World on Fire* (Paulist, 2017).
18 René Terranova, *Manual de Guerra Espiritual* (Casa Creación, 2006).
19 Romero, *Violence of Love.*
20 Ivone Gebara, *Out of the Depths: Women's Experience of Evil and Salvation* (Fortress, 2002).
21 Gutiérrez, *We Drink from Our Own Wells.*
22 Eduardo Galeano, *Open Veins of Latin America: Five Centuries of the Pillage of a Continent* (Monthly Review, 1997).
23 Miguel A. De La Torre, *Embracing Hopelessness* (Fortress, 2017).

24 Samuel Solivan, *The Spirit, Pathos, and Liberation: Toward an Hispanic Pentecostal Theology* (Sheffield Academic, 1998).
25 Solivan, *The Spirit, Pathos, and Liberation.*
26 Loida I. Martell-Otero, Zaida Maldonado Pérez, and Elizabeth Conde-Frazier, *Latina Evangélicas: A Theological Survey from the Margins* (Cascade, 2013).

Chapter Four—Majesty

1 Karl Barth, *Church Dogmatics: The Doctrine of Reconciliation*, vol. 4, part 2: *Jesus Christ, the Servant as Lord*, trans. Geoffrey William Bromiley (Bloomsbury, 2004).
2 Hans Urs von Balthasar, *The Glory of the Lord: A Theological Aesthetics* (T&T Clark, 1982).
3 Jürgen Moltmann, *The Crucified God: The Cross of Christ as the Foundation and Criticism of Christian Theology* (SCM, 1974).
4 Richard Griswold del Castillo and Richard A. Garcia, *César Chávez: A Triumph of Spirit* (University of Oklahoma, 1995).
5 Óscar Romero, *The Church Is All of You: Thoughts of Archbishop Óscar Romero* (Harper Collins, 1984).
6 Garcilaso de la Vega, *The Florida of the Inca*, trans. and ed. John Grier Varner and Jeanette Johnson Varner (University of Texas Press, 1962).
7 Steven Payne, *The Carmelite Tradition* (Liturgical, 2011).
8 Teresa of Ávila, *The Way of Perfection*, trans. E. Allison Peers (Image, 1964).
9 E. Allison Peers, *The Mysticism of St. Teresa of Avila* (Faber and Faber, 1951).
10 Caroline Walker Bynum, *Holy Feast and Holy Fast: The Religious Significance of Food to Medieval Women* (University of California, 1987).
11 Teresa of Ávila, *The Interior Castle*, trans. E. Allison Peers (Image, 1961).
12 Elizondo, *Galilean Journey*; Orlando O. Espín, *The Faith of the People: Theological Reflections on Popular Catholicism* (Orbis, 1997).
13 Peers, *Mysticism of St. Teresa of Avila.*
14 Peers, *Mysticism of St. Teresa of Avila.*
15 Teresa of Ávila, *The Life of St. Teresa of Avila by Herself*, trans. J. M. Cohen (Penguin, 1957).
16 Teresa of Ávila, *The Collected Works of St. Teresa of Avila*, vol. 1, trans. Kieran Kavanaugh and Otilio Rodriguez (ICS, 1976).
17 de la Vega, *Florida of the Inca.*
18 Antonio Vieira, *Sermões*, vol. 1, ed. Alcir Pécora (Editora Hedra, 2000).
19 Alexander Schmemann, *For the Life of the World: Sacraments and Orthodoxy* (St. Vladimir's Seminary, 1973).
20 Richard Rohr, *The Universal Christ: How a Forgotten Reality Can Change Everything We See, Hope For, and Believe* (Convergent, 2019).

Chapter Five—Piety

1 Toribio de Benavente Motolinía, *Historia de los indios de la Nueva España*, ed. Edmundo O'Gorman (Porrúa, 1951); Bartolomé de las Casas, *A Short Account of the Destruction of the Indies*, trans. Nigel Griffin (Penguin Classics, 1992).
2 Robert Chao Romero and Marcos Canales, eds., *Las Casas on Faithful Witness* (Samuel Morris, 2022).
3 Bartolomé de las Casas, *In Defense of the Indians* (Northern Illinois University Press, 1992).
4 Gustavo Gutiérrez, *Las Casas: In Search of the Poor of Jesus Christ*, trans. Robert R. Barr (Orbis, 1993).
5 de las Casas, *Short Account of the Destruction of the Indies.*
6 de las Casas, *In Defense of the Indians.*
7 The encomienda system, a Spanish labor system that granted colonists the right to demand forced labor from Indigenous people, was heavily criticized by Bartolomé de las Casas after his personal transformation. See de las Casas, *Short Account of the Destruction of the Indies*, 12–14.
8 Romero and Canales, *Las Casas on Faithful Witness.*
9 John of the Cross, *Dark Night of the Soul.*

Chapter Six—Solitude

1 Natalia Imperatori-Lee Reyes, *Cuéntame: Narrative in the Ecclesial Present* (Orbis, 2018).
2 Paulo Freire, *Pedagogy of the Oppressed* (Bloomsbury, 1970).
3 John of the Cross, *Ascent of Mount Carmel*, book 1, chap. 13, sec. 11, in *The Collected Works of St. John of the Cross*, trans. Kieran Kavanaugh and Otilio Rodriguez (ICS Publications, 1991), 132.
4 John of the Cross, *The Spiritual Canticle* (1622).
5 Other Latino theologians such as Virgilio Elizondo and Orlando Espín have engaged deeply with the mystical theology of Juan de la Cruz. See Elizondo, *Galilean Journey*; and Espín, *Faith of the People.*
6 John of the Cross, *St. John of the Cross: The Living Flame of Love: Study Edition* (ICS Publications, 2023).
7 Baltasar Gracián, *The Art of Worldly Wisdom*, trans. Christopher Maurer (Doubleday, 1992).
8 Merton, *New Seeds of Contemplation.*
9 Randy Harris, *Soul Work: Confessions of a Part-Time Monk* (Leafwood Publishers, 2011).
10 Jackie L. Halstead, *Leaning Into God's Embrace: A Guidebook for Contemplative Prayer* (Leafwood Publishers, 2021).
11 Gracián, *Art of Worldly Wisdom.*
12 Jeremy Robbins, *Arts of Perception: The Epistemological Mentality of the Spanish Baroque, 1580–1720* (Routledge, 2007).
13 Francisco de Vitoria, *Political Writings*, ed. Anthony Pagden and Jeremy Lawrence (Cambridge University Press, 1991); Anthony Pagden, *Las Casas and the Defense of the*

Americas (University of Chicago Press, 1993); Luis de Molina, *On Divine Foreknowledge: Part IV of the Concordia*, trans. Alfred J. Freddoso (Cornell University Press, 1988).

14 Teresa of Ávila, *The Interior Castle*; María de Ágreda, *The Mystical City of God*, trans. Fiscar Marison (TAN, 2009); Juana Inés de la Cruz, *Poems, Protest, and a Dream*, trans. Margaret Sayers Peden (Penguin, 1997).

15 Thomas Merton, *Thoughts in Solitude* (Farrar, Straus and Cudahy, 1958).

Chapter Seven—Rectitude

1 Gutiérrez, *We Drink from Our Own Wells*; Sobrino, *Jesus the Liberator.*

2 Bartolomé de las Casas, *Bartolomé de las Casas: An Essay in Spanish Historiography* (University Florida Press, 1954).

3 Miguel Hidalgo y Costilla, *The Oxford History of Mexico*, ed. Michael C. Meyer and William H. Beezley (Oxford University Press, 2000).

4 Luis Tapia Rubio, "Bartolomé de las Casas's Coloniality as a Warning for the Christian Mission in Latin America," *Journal of Latin American Theology* 19, no. 1 (2024): 11–33.

5 Judy Baca, *The Great Wall of Los Angeles*, 1974–83, Mural (Los Angeles, California).

6 Samuel Escobar, *Changing Tides: Latin America and World Mission Today* (Orbis Books, 2002).

7 René Padilla and Tetsunao Yamamori, eds., *The New Face of Evangelicalism: An International Symposium on the Lausanne Covenant* (Hodder & Stoughton, 1976).

8 Samuel Escobar, *Evangelical Theology in Latin America: The Contextual Nature of Theology* (Ediciones Certeza, 1992).

9 James Martin, *Mi vida con los santos* (Loyola Press, 2010), 79.

10 Ignacio de Loyola, *Personal Writings: Reminiscences, Spiritual Diary, Select Letters including the Text of the Spiritual Exercises*, trans. Joseph A. Munitiz and Philip Endean (Penguin, 1996).

11 Ignacio de Loyola, *The Spiritual Exercises of St. Ignacio*, trans. Louis J. Puhl (Loyola, 1951).

12 W. W. Meissner, *Ignacio de Loyola: The Psychology of a Saint* (Yale University Press, 1992).

13 John W. O'Malley, *The First Jesuits* (Harvard University Press, 1993).

14 George E. Ganss, *The Jesuit Order as a Synagogue of Jews: Jesuits of Jewish Ancestry and Purity-of-Blood Laws in the Early Society of Jesus* (Brill, 2009).

15 *Monumenta Historica Societatis Iesu (MHSI), Epistolae et Instructiones*, vol. 1 (Successores Rivadeneyra, 1903). For more on the early Jesuits and how expressions like "Ite, inflammate omnia" became paraphrased in Jesuit tradition, see John W. O'Malley, *The First Jesuits* (Harvard University Press, 1993; various reprints), and *The Jesuits: A History from Ignatius to the Present* (Rowman & Littlefield, 2014). O'Malley does not confirm the exact phrase "Go forth and set the world on fire" but discusses how such mottoes arose from Ignatian ideals.

16 For more on the impact of Ignatius on Catholic mission, see Jonathan Wright, *The Jesuits: Missions, Myths and Histories* (HarperCollins, 2004).

17 Miguel Hidalgo y Costilla, Michael C. Meyer, and William H. Beezley, *The Oxford History of Mexico* (Oxford University Press, 2000).

18 Justo L. González and Ondina E. González, *Christianity in Latin America: A History* (Cambridge University Press, 2007).
19 Hidalgo y Costilla, Meyer, and Beezley, *Oxford History of Mexico.*
20 Luis Pérez Aguirre, *La opción entrañable ante los despojados de sus derechos* (Editorial Sal Terrae, 1992), 116.
21 Camilo Maccise, *En el invierno eclesial: Luces y sombras de una experiencia* (Penguin Random House, 2015).
22 Shifra M. Goldman, *Dimensions of the Americas: Art and Social Change in Latin America and the United States* (University of Chicago Press, 1994).
23 Dietrich Bonhoeffer, *Ethics* (Touchstone, 1995).
24 Sobrino, *Jesus the Liberator.*

Chapter Eight—Noble Majesty, Sacred Piety, Vulnerable Solitude, and Just Rectitude

1 "68 VOCES," November 2020, 68voces.mx, https://68voces.mx/.
2 Ignacio Ellacuría, "The Historicity of Christian Salvation," in *Mysterium Liberationis: Fundamental Concepts of Liberation Theology*, ed. Ignacio Ellacuría and Jon Sobrino (Orbis Books, 1993), 369–70.
3 Ada María Isasi-Díaz, *En la lucha / In the Struggle: Elaborating a Mujerista Theology* (Fortress Press, 2004), 200.
4 Espín, *Faith of the People.*
5 Fernando F. Segovia, *Decolonizing Biblical Studies: A View from the Margins* (Orbis Books, 2000).
6 María Pilar Aquino, *Our Cry for Life: Feminist Theology from Latin America* (Orbis Books, 1993).
7 Ignacio Ellacuría, "The Challenge of the Poor to the Christian Faith," in *Freedom Made Flesh: The Mission of the Church in Latin America*, trans. Margaret Wilde (UCA Editors, 1975), 48.
8 Clarissa Pinkola Estés, *Women Who Run with the Wolves: Myths and Stories of the Wild Woman Archetype* (Random House, 1989).
9 Ignacio Ellacuría, *Filosofía de la Realidad Histórica* (Trotta, 1991).
10 Ignacio Ellacuría, "The Praxis of Liberation and Christian Faith," in *Theology in the Americas*, ed. Sergio Torres and Virginia Fabella (Orbis Books, 1976), 175.
11 Ignacio Ellacuría, "Crucified Peoples: An Essay in Historical Soteriology," *Concilium* 188 (1986): 92.
12 Samin Nosrat, *Salt, Fat, Acid, Heat: Mastering the Elements of Good Cooking* (Simon & Schuster, 2017).
13 Alexander Golitzin, *Mystagogy: A Monastic Reading of Dionysius Areopagita* (Liturgical, 2014).
14 Maximus, *On the Ecclesiastical Mystagogy* (St. Vladimir's Seminary, 2019).
15 Segovia, *Decolonizing Biblical Studies.*
16 Paul van Geest, *Seeing through the Eyes of Faith: New Approaches to the Mystagogy of the Church Fathers* (Peeters, 2016); Saint Ambrose, *On the Mysteries*, trans. Roy J. Deferrari (The Catholic University of America, 1963); and Saint Augustine, *The City of God.*

17 Christopher J. Paradise and A. Malcolm Campbell, *Organismal Homeostasis* (Momentum, 2016).
18 Ignacio Ellacuría, "The Sacrament of Liberation," *Diakonía* 19, no. 2 (1984): 32.
19 Cyril of Jerusalem, *Mystagogic Catechesis III* ("On Chrism"), § 3, in *Nicene and Post-Nicene Fathers*, 2nd ser., vol. 7, *Cyril of Jerusalem: Catechetical Lectures*, ed. Philip Schaff and Henry Wace, trans. Edwin Hamilton Gifford (Hendrickson, 1994), 150.
20 Ignacio Ellacuría, "Utopía y profetismo desde América Latina," in *Escritos teológicos*, vol. 4 (San Salvador: UCA Editores, 2000), 226.

Chapter Nine—Cultivating the Spiritual Feast in Christian Communities

1 Wilmer Estrada-Carrasquillo, *Beyond the Temple: Pentecostal Spirituality as a Lived Ecclesiology* (CPT Press, 2021).
2 See Ignacio Ellacuría, *Essays on History, Liberation, and Salvation* (Orbis, 2013).
3 Jon Sobrino and Juan Pico Hernández, *Theology of Christian Solidarity* (Orbis, 1985).
4 Sammy Alfaro, *Divino Compañero: Toward a Hispanic Pentecostal Christology* (Wipf & Stock, 2010).
5 Sobrino, *Christology at the Crossroads.*
6 Enrique Dussel, *Ethics of Liberation: In the Age of Globalization and Exclusion* (Duke University Press, 2013).
7 Ronald G. Musto, *Liberation Theologies: A Research Guide* (Taylor & Francis, 2020).
8 Christopher Warnes and Kim Anderson Sasser, eds., *Magical Realism and Literature* (Cambridge University Press, 2020).
9 Ana María Pineda, *Rutilio Grande: Memory and Legacy of a Jesuit Martyr* (Lectio Publishing, 2022).
10 Mercedes Sosa, "Gracias a la Vida," track 1 on *Homenaje a Violeta Parra*, PolyGram Records, 1971, MP3.
11 Taizé Community, *Wait for the Lord* (Ateliers et Presses de Taizé, 1998), MP3.
12 Stephen J. Pope, ed., *Hope and Solidarity: Jon Sobrino's Challenge to Christian Theology* (Orbis, 2015).
13 Ronald Rolheiser, *The Holy Longing: The Search for a Christian Spirituality* (Doubleday, 1999).
14 W. John Green, *A History of Political Murder in Latin America: Killing the Messengers of Change* (SUNY Press, 2015).